D1029289

*The Pan-American Federation of Labor*

# The Pan-American Federation of Labor

*Sinclair Snow*

*Duke University Press*
*Durham, North Carolina*
1964

331.88
Sy6

# Preface

Except for comments in general works, there have been only
two attempts to deal with the Pan-American Federation of
Labor. The first was a hundred-page pamphlet by Ya. Vilenkin entitled *Panamerikanskaya federatsiya truda,* which was
published in Moscow in 1929. This is an analysis of the Pan-
American Federation of Labor from the Soviet point of view.
Based on the *Proceedings* of the various congresses of the organization beginning in 1918 and ending in 1927, Vilenkin's
pamphlet condemns the Pan-American Federation of Labor
as a device of United States imperialism to control or destroy
militant trade unionism in Latin America, and it predicted
that because of its reactionary nature the organization could
not survive.

A later study based on both the *Proceedings* and the *American Federationist,* the official organ of the American Federation of Labor, is a paper by Charles M. Toth, a graduate
student at the University of Illinois, entitled "The Pan-American Federation of Labor." This unpublished manuscript of
some thirty pages was written as a Master of Arts thesis in
1947. In 1958 a summary of this paper appeared in the *Re-
vista de Ciencias Sociales,* a publication of the University of
Puerto Rico, under the title of "La Federación Pan-Americana del Trabajo: su naturaleza política." In both his thesis
and in his summary Mr. Toth makes a number of errors
which detract from the worth of his paper.

Brief mention of the Pan-American Federation of Labor
is made in various works, including Samuel Gompers, *Sev-*

*enty Years of Life and Labor;* Philip Taft, *The A. F. of L. in the Time of Gompers;* Louis S. Reed, *The Labor Philosophy of Samuel Gompers;* Moisés Poblete Troncoso, *El movimiento obrero latinoamericano;* Moisés Poblete Troncoso and Ben G. Burnett, *The Rise of the Latin American Labor Movement;* Alfonso López Aparicio, *El movimiento obrero en México;* and Lewis S. Lorwin, *Labor and Internationalism.* The views of Taft and of Reed as to why the Pan-American Federation of Labor failed to survive are especially interesting. Taft believes that the death of Samuel Gompers was the greatest factor contributing to its failure, for Gompers had been its prime support and inspiration. Reed takes a somewhat different point of view and states that except for the work that it did in relation to Mexico, the organization was largely unsuccessful from the beginning. Marc Karson in his *American Labor Unions and Politics: 1900-1918,* which should have at least mentioned the Pan-American Federation of Labor, passes it over in silence but at the same time comments on the unwillingness of Gompers to protect the Latin-American workers from United States imperialism. This is an opinion held by many persons, but a thorough study of Gompers and his Latin-American policy will show that it is far from valid. Whatever the outcome of his efforts, it cannot be denied that Gompers made a sincere effort to aid the people of Latin America.

The relation of organized labor in the United States to Latin America has been poorly understood because of the lack of printed material dealing with the subject. The author hopes that the relationship will be clarified by this study, which has been based upon the correspondence between the leaders of the Pan-American labor movement. This material is widely scattered, some of it being in private hands in Mexico and Puerto Rico, while the greater part of it is in Bancroft Library, the Library of Congress, the National Archives, and the files of the American Federation of Labor—Congress of

Industrial Organizations. What appears to be part of the files of the Pan-American Federation of Labor is contained in the papers of the late Senator Santiago Iglesias Pantín of Puerto Rico. The greatest amount of material is in the Gompers Copybooks and in a collection of microfilmed letters and documents relating to Gompers, both of which are in the AFL-CIO files in Washington. Fortunately for the historian, Gompers frequently summarized in the opening paragraph of each of his replies the essence of the communication to which he referred. This makes some of the footnotes puzzling, but it also makes it possible to fill gaps in the story of the Pan-American Federation of Labor which would otherwise remain unfilled.

Several persons have contributed to the publication of this book. The author wishes to acknowledge the assistance of Dr. C. Alan Hutchinson, associate professor of history in the University of Virginia; Mrs. Ethel Duffy Turner, author of *Ricardo Flores Magón y el Partido Liberal* and widow of John Kenneth Turner, author of *Barbarous Mexico;* Mrs. Igualdad Iglesias de Pagán, daughter of Santiago Iglesias and widow of the Puerto Rican statesman and historian Bolívar Pagán; Mrs. Eloise Giles, formerly librarian for the AFL-CIO at its national headquarters; Mr. Logan Kimmel, archivist for the AFL-CIO; and Miss Vicki Wilson of Walhalla, South Carolina.

*Lander College*
*Greenwood, South Carolina*
*February 29, 1964*

# Contents

*The Pan-American Federation of Labor*

# One. The AFL-Mexican Labor Conference

The Pan-American Federation of Labor was organized to protect the working people of the Western Hemisphere, especially those of Latin America, from predatory capital, although in practice the organization departed from its original purpose by dealing with social and political problems as well as those of an economic nature. This was no doubt due to the broad views of its founders, the best-known of whom were John Murray, an American revolutionist; Santiago Iglesias Pantín, a Spanish-born Puerto Rican leftist; and Samuel Gompers, the liberal founder of the American Federation of Labor.

Samuel Gompers first became acquainted with Latin-American problems through a small group of anti-Díaz Mexican cigarmakers with whom he worked in New York during the 1880's.[1] Many years later, after he had become a person of prominence in American life, more and more representatives of the Mexican revolutionary movement came to confer with him. Among others, he was in touch with Ricardo Flores Magón,[2] the leader of the Mexican Liberal party, which had established headquarters in the United States in 1904. In 1907, when Flores Magón and other leaders of the Liberal party were arrested by United States authorities, Gompers was instrumental in preventing their extradition to Mexico,[3]

---

1. Samuel Gompers, *Seventy Years of Life and Labor: An Autobiography* (New York, 1925), II, 303.
2. *Ibid.*, 306.
3. Grace Heilman Stimson, *Rise of the Labor Movement in Los Angeles* (Berkeley and Los Angeles, 1955), p. 321.

where they would undoubtedly have been condemned to death or to long terms in prison for the activities they had carried on against President Porfirio Díaz of Mexico. At the Denver convention of the American Federation of Labor in 1908, Gompers was successful in getting his followers to adopt a resolution demanding the freedom of Ricardo Flores Magón, Antonio I. Villarreal, and Librado Rivera, the leaders of the Mexican Liberal party who had been imprisoned in the United States for the alleged violation of certain United States neutrality acts.[4] Despite the efforts of Gompers to have these men set free, they remained in prison, and in 1910, when they again appealed to him for aid, he continued to give them support.[5]

Following the Mexican Revolution of 1910 which overthrew Porfirio Díaz, there was a growing fear on the part of many Mexican revolutionists that the United States would aid the counterrevolution which had developed in Mexico. These fears were well-founded, for antilabor businessmen in the United States had invested large sums in Mexican factories, mines, railroads, oil fields, and other enterprises during the Díaz period. These investments had paid well while Díaz was in control, but they had suffered during the Revolution and there was reason to believe that they would lose much if not all of their value if the Revolution were allowed to continue. Businessmen longed for the days when their investments had been secure, and they put pressure on President William Howard Taft to intervene in the struggle. Precisely what should be done was not made clear, but by the fall of 1912 there was much sentiment in the United States for intervention of some kind. In a move to forestall such action, Lázaro Gutiérrez de Lara, a prominent follower

4. Samuel Gompers, "United States-Mexican Labor: Their Relations," *American Federationist*, Aug. 1916, p. 7.
5. Samuel Gompers to William B. Cleary, Jan. 24, 1910; in the Gompers Copybooks, hereinafter abbreviated GCB, which are on file at the national headquarters of the American Federation of Labor—Congress of Industrial Organizations in Washington, D. C.

of Mexican President Francisco I. Madero and a former leader in the Mexican Liberal party, appealed in person to the Executive Council of the American Federation of Labor. De Lara was acting as the representative of a commission of Mexican revolutionists who had been sent to the United States for the specific purpose of appealing to the AFL to protest publicly against what was generally believed in Mexican revolutionary circles to be a plan for United States military intervention in Mexico. The Executive Council, after hearing the appeal of de Lara, decided in favor of the protest,[6] but what action, if any, was taken as a result of this decision is not clear.

The worst fears of the Mexican revolutionists were realized in February 1913 when a counterrevolutionary group, with the encouragement and possibly the aid of the United States ambassador to Mexico, Henry Lane Wilson, engineered a successful revolt that culminated in the murders of President Madero and Vice-president José María Pino Suárez. Victoriano Huerta, Madero's leading general—who had made the revolt a success by betraying his commander-in-chief—was appointed provisional president by the counterrevolutionists. The Taft government did not recognize the Huerta regime, despite the urging of Henry Lane Wilson, but the new ruler was soon formally accepted by the leading nations of the world except for the United States. When Woodrow Wilson took office in March 1913, he lost no time in making clear his position in regard to the counterrevolution. Within a matter of days after his inauguration, he had stated that he would not recognize the government of Victoriano Huerta, and by the end of the year he had won the major powers to his point of view. Strong opposition to Huerta had arisen throughout Mexico from the day of his accession to power, and this was especially true in the northern part of the coun-

6. Memorandum by Santiago Iglesias, dated 1912; in the Iglesias Papers, hereinafter abbreviated IP, which are in the possession of Mrs. Igualdad Iglesias de Pagán of Santurce, Puerto Rico.

try, where Governor Venustiano Carranza of Coahuila had organized a movement to restore constitutional government according to the plans of Madero. President Wilson, by lifting the embargo on arms for Mexico, allowed Carranza and other enemies of Huerta to receive a plentiful supply of weapons and ammunition from the United States. Huerta soon began to lose ground, and a few months after the capture and occupation of Veracruz by United States military forces in April 1914, he resigned the presidency and went into exile. Mexico then came under the nominal control of Venustiano Carranza.

News of Huerta's resignation had hardly reached Washington before Gompers began to work for peace in Mexico. After consulting the Executive Council, he wrote a long letter to Rafael Zubarán Capmany, Carranza's representative in the United States, in which he praised Madero and expressed admiration for the aims of the Revolution. He told Zubarán that inasmuch as the AFL had supported the Revolution and had opposed Huerta, it had the right to suggest that the conflict be brought to a close by granting amnesty to those *huertistas* still under arms and by adopting a policy of dividing the large landed estates among the landless peons.[7] Soon after this letter was written, Carranza entered Mexico City and it no doubt appeared to Gompers that the fighting would soon be over. At the annual convention of the AFL in November following these events, Gompers succeeded in having a resolution adopted recognizing the Carranza government.[8]

In June 1915 Gompers became acquainted with an American revolutionist who was intimately associated with the Mexican revolutionary movement and the forces behind

7. Gompers to Rafael Zubarán, July 25, 1914; in a microfilmed collection of papers to, from, and concerning Samuel Gompers, hereinafter abbreviated GM, which are on file at AFL-CIO headquarters.
8. *Proceedings* of the Thirty-fourth Annual Convention of the American Federation of Labor, November 9-12, 1914, pp. 50-52; hereinafter cited as *Proceedings*, 34th AFL Conv.

Carranza. This man was John Murray, a philanthropic individual who had for many years been promoting the welfare of mankind in general and that of the Mexican poor of California in particular. Murray, a member of the Quaker family for which Murray Hill in New York City was named, had established himself in California some years before the Mexican Revolution in the hope that the climate there would improve his health. In his youth he had been greatly influenced by the writings of Leo Tolstoy and later, having decided to devote his life to the cause of human progress, he had refused his patrimony and had become active in behalf of the Mexican laborers, the "wet-backs" of his day, in California. In time he became an active socialist and a friend of many revolutionists, reformers, and trade unionists, both Mexican and American, on the West Coast and in the East. A competent editor as well as writer, Murray had been associated with several radical newspapers, including the Los Angeles *Citizen,* the Tucson *Border,* and the Washington, D. C., *Pan-American Press.* He had been jailed on a false charge of conspiring to murder President William Howard Taft on the occasion of his meeting with President Porfirio Díaz on the International Bridge over the Rio Grande at El Paso, Texas. Through his friend Job Harriman, a noted labor lawyer who had defended the Liberal party leaders in 1907, he met many persons associated with this radical group. In 1908, with credentials supplied by Ricardo Flores Magón, he made a trip to Mexico City and other towns in central Mexico. Flores Magón described him as "an American newspaperman of advanced ideas."[9] The object of this trip is not clear, but it was no doubt connected with the anti-Díaz activities of the Mexican Liberal party. Some years later Murray became associated with the New York *Call,* the daily organ of the Social-

9. Quoted from an unpublished biographical sketch of John Murray written by his friend and colleague, Mrs. Ethel Duffy Turner, hereinafter referred to as John Murray MS.

ist party, and late in February 1915, with credentials from the *Call*, he sailed from New York to Veracruz.[10] Ostensibly his mission was that of a newspaperman in search of material on the Revolution for his paper, but subsequent events suggest that his real purpose was to lay the basis for closer cooperation between the organized labor movements of the United States and Mexico. Whether he took this action on his own initiative or at the suggestion of some other person is not clear.

Conditions in Mexico at the time of Murray's arrival there were chaotic. Fighting had broken out the preceding fall between the Constitutionalists and the supporters of the Convention of Aguascalientes, and Carranza had been forced to abandon Mexico City for Veracruz. The capital changed hands several times during this period, and the Conventionists, first under the leadership of Eulalio Gutiérrez and later Roque González Garza, were shifting back and forth from Mexico City to Cuernavaca as the military situation demanded. In mid-March, about the time that Murray arrived in Veracruz, the capital had again come under the control of the Conventionists. The future of the Constitutionalists at this time was not bright, but after the defeat of Pancho Villa by Alvaro Obregón at Celaya in April 1915 the fortunes of Carranza began to improve.

The activities of Murray during his visit are only partly known, but it is clear that he visited Mexico City and a number of other towns and that he conferred with many Mexican labor leaders, intellectuals, and political figures. From them he obtained documents relating to the recent alliance between Carranza and the Casa del Obrero Mundial,[11] a revolutionary federation of trade unions organized in 1912 which had in its leadership several persons connected

10. New York *Call*, March 1, 1915.
11. John Murray MS.

with the Mexican Liberal party.[12] The Casa del Obrero Mundial welcomed Murray's visit and showed its confidence in him by making him a member of its Comité Revolucionario.[13]

When Murray returned to the United States in the late spring of 1915, he was convinced that the time had come for an alliance between the organized labor movements of the United States and Mexico. In Washington, through mutual friends, he met Santiago Iglesias Pantín of Puerto Rico,[14] who had arrived at the same conclusion. Iglesias, a Spaniard by birth, had been the general organizer for the AFL in Puerto Rico since 1901. A Marxist like John Murray, Iglesias had organized the Partido Socialista de Puerto Rico for political action, and for economic action he had organized the Federación Libre de los Trabajadores de Puerto Rico, which was affiliated with the AFL. Despite the socialist views of Iglesias, Gompers held him in high esteem and for many years depended upon him as his chief aide and spokesman in Latin-American and especially Caribbean affairs. The leader in progressive thought in Puerto Rican labor circles for many years, Iglesias was the Resident Commissioner in Washington for Puerto Rico at the time of his death in 1939.[15]

The first meeting between Murray and Iglesias took place shortly after the conclusion of the Pan-American Financial and Trade Conference of 1915. This conference, which was held under the auspices of the Pan American Union, was of sufficient importance to require an address by President Wilson at its opening session on May 25. When it terminated its sessions three weeks later, it had laid the basis for closer

12. Alfonso López Aparicio, *El movimiento obrero en México: antecedentes, desarrollo y tendencias* (México, 1952), pp. 151-152.
13. John Murray MS.
14. Santiago Iglesias, "Recuerdo de John Murray," *Justicia* (San Juan, P. R.), 19 de enero de 1920, p. 5.
15. Gompers to Santiago Iglesias, May 19, 1916; GCB. Conrado Ansejo, ed., *Quien es quien en Puerto Rico* (San Juan, P. R., 1933-34), p. 88. Further

business co-operation between the United States and nations to the south. Iglesias had been present at two sessions of the conference as an observer and had discussed it with several delegates from Latin America.[16] He believed that the conference would lead to action that would be detrimental to the welfare of the working people of Latin America, and he felt that the situation called for a counterorganization of Pan-American labor.[17] Moreover, he saw that Murray's plan for closer co-operation between United States and Mexican labor could be expanded to include all of Latin America and thus meet the threat of organized Pan-American capital.

Following his conference with Murray, Iglesias made a report to Gompers which went briefly as follows: Murray called to see Iglesias at the latter's hotel room in Washington. They discussed Mexican affairs and Murray showed Iglesias pictures, posters, newspapers, and documents regarding the labor and revolutionary movements in Mexico. Among this material was a copy of a proclamation issued by Carranza and posted in Orizaba, Veracruz, and other Mexican cities saying that an agreement had been reached between Carranza and the Casa del Obrero Mundial in which Carranza agreed that in return for the support of the Casa del Obrero Mundial against the anti-Carranza factions he would guarantee that the rights of workers would be protected, that better working conditions would be assured, that labor legislation would be enacted, that meeting places would be provided for the unions, and that the Casa del Obrero Mundial would be free to hold meetings in its own halls without molestation. Murray explained to Iglesias that the Mexican labor movement was radical because of its Spanish origin and that it was in reality an integral part of the Revolution itself.

information on Iglesias prior to 1915 is contained in his autobiographical *Luchas emancipadores* (San Juan de Puerto Rico, 1958, second printing).

16. Santiago Iglesias, "Recuerdo de John Murray," *Justicia*, 19 de enero de 1920, p. 5.

17. Statement made by Organizer Santiago Iglesias to President Gompers on Mexican Relations, Washington, June 10, 1915; GM.

Murray insisted that the AFL should take the initiative in getting in touch with the organized labor movement in Mexico. He suggested that a commission representing the AFL be sent to Mexico to determine for itself the conditions existing there and to confer with the leaders of Mexican labor as to the steps to be taken in forming an AFL-Mexican labor alliance. After having heard this report, Iglesias suggested that Murray confer with Gompers, but as the latter was absent from Washington at this time, Murray and Iglesias held an informal meeting with James Lord, the head of the Mining Department of the AFL and later an officer of the Pan-American Federation of Labor, and a small group of high officials of the AFL who were permanently located in Washington. Iglesias closed his report to Gompers by pointing out the relationship between Murray's suggestion for a closer tie between the AFL and Mexican labor and the recent activities of the Pan-American Financial Congress.[18]

Shortly after this meeting, Iglesias introduced Murray to Gompers.[19] Gompers had known of Murray's work in the Political Refugee Defense League,[20] an organization in which Gompers was also interested. Many years later Gompers revealed that Murray had been suspicious of him because of his attitude toward the socialist movement,[21] and that in 1909 when Murray was jailed in connection with the Taft-Díaz meeting,[22] Murray had appealed for aid to Congressman William B. Wilson, the AFL leader who later became President Wilson's Secretary of Labor, rather than to Gompers.[23] Mur-

18. *Ibid.* Canuto A. Vargas in "El legado de John Murray," *Justicia*, 1 de noviembre de 1920, p. 11, says that in the fall of 1917, when Murray was in Arizona in connection with a strike among the Mexican miners, Murray had told him of his plan for a Pan-American labor federation to counteract organized capital with government support, which "was swallowing up Latin America, even beyond Mexico."
19. Iglesias to Ramón Martínez, Aug. 4, 1915; IP.
20. Gompers, *Seventy Years of Life and Labor,* II, 308.
21. *Ibid.*
22. A number of documents relating to the Murray case are to be found indexed under "John Murray" in the Justice Department files in the National Archives.
23. Gompers, *Seventy Years of Life and Labor,* II, 308.

ray's suspicion of Gompers was dispelled at their meeting in 1915 and from that time until Murray's death in 1919 they worked closely together. Murray, like all persons who came in contact with Gompers, was strongly attracted by the personality of "the Chief," as he was called by his close associates, and Gompers in turn was impressed with the depth of Murray's character. Gompers immediately accepted Murray as his chief aide and advisor in Mexican affairs,[24] and Murray easily convinced him, as he had convinced Iglesias, that the AFL should enter into some kind of formal alliance with Mexican labor and that Gompers should without delay urge President Wilson to recognize the Carranza government. Gompers immediately took steps in this direction and a flow of correspondence between Gompers and various individuals in Mexico began.

By June 1915 the Mexican trade unionists, now supporters of Carranza, saw that victory for the Constitutionalists was near. But the Wilson government showed no signs of giving its support to Carranza. To the contrary, there were strong indications that the United States would intervene to bring the conflict to a close by imposing on Mexico a compromise president chosen by the Wilson government. Fear of intervention led the Comité Revolucionario of the Veracruz branch of the Casa del Obrero Mundial to send to Gompers a telegram protesting against intervention and assuring him that in such an event the trade unionists of Mexico would continue to fight for the Carranza faction.[25] Gompers was absent from Washington when this telegram arrived,[26] but on his return he hastened to send to President Wilson a translation of the telegram, and in a long letter he outlined for Wilson the Mexican situation essentially as Murray had explained it to Iglesias and presumably as Murray had related

24. Santiago Iglesias, "Recuerdo de John Murray," *Justicia*, 19 de enero de 1920, p. 5.
25. Casa del Obrero Mundial to Gompers, June 10, 1915; GCB and IP.
26. Gompers to Rafael Quintero, June 18, 1915; GM.

it to Gompers.[27] Gompers then wrote to Rafael Quintero, the secretary of the Casa del Obrero Mundial in Veracruz, of the action that he had taken.[28]

A month later Gompers received a wire from Joaquín Correa, the secretary of the Confederación de Sindicatos Obreros de la República Mexicana, which asked Gompers to protest reports in the United States press which were casting aspersions on the Revolution by portraying Mexico as a land of starvation.[29] There was some basis for these reports, especially in relation to Mexico City, but they were undoubtedly grossly exaggerated and could serve as a pretext for United States intervention as a humanitarian move. Gompers complied with the request of Correa by communicating the message to President Wilson and suggesting that the alleged food shortage in Mexico might warrant an investigation by some qualified, reliable person.[30]

The willingness of Gompers to speak for Mexican labor led to further requests from that quarter. In early August, Gompers received a long letter from Edmundo E. Martínez, a special envoy of the Mexican labor movement to the United States. In his letter Martínez explained that he had been chosen at a meeting of the Mexican Federation of Labor[31] in Veracruz to go to the United States because American newspapers distorted news from Mexico and because the time had come for more friendly relations between the United States and Mexico. Martínez praised Carranza for his support of organized labor and he condemned Pancho Villa and Emiliano Zapata for prolonging the civil war. He insisted that Carranza was the genuine leader of Mexican democracy, and

27. Gompers to Woodrow Wilson, June 14, 1915; IP and GCB.
28. Gompers to Rafael Quintero, June 18, 1915; IP.
29. Federación de Sindicatos Obreros to Gompers, July 9, 1915; GCB.
30. Gompers to Woodrow Wilson, July 17, 1915; GM and GCB.
31. The "Mexican Federation of Labor" here referred to is probably the Federación de Sindicatos Obreros branch in Veracruz. In later years the name was applied exclusively to the Confederación Regional Obrera Mexicana. See Gompers to Woodrow Wilson, July 21, 1915; GCB.

he asked Gompers for moral aid in getting the United States to recognize the Carranza government.[32]

Shortly after this letter a meeting between Gompers and Martínez was held.[33] Immediately following this meeting, Gompers wrote President Wilson of the event and sent him a copy of a letter that he had received from Martínez regarding recognition. Wilson was at this time vacationing in New Hampshire, but Gompers was so impressed with the revelations of Martínez that he wanted Wilson to grant Martínez an interview without delay. While apologizing to Wilson for breaking in on his vacation, Gompers said that Martínez, who spoke English well, would be happy to make the trip to New Hampshire if for only a half-hour audience.[34] In his anxiety to have Martínez lay the Mexican question directly before the President, Gompers wired him in advance of the important letter that he was sending him.[35] After he had received the letter, Wilson replied that while he could not grant Martínez an interview, his attitude toward Mexico would be influenced by the letter from Martínez to Gompers.[36] Gompers evidently believed that Wilson would discuss the Mexican problem with Martínez, and he had possibly intimated this in a letter to the latter, for soon after this event he wrote Martínez a soothing letter to the effect that Wilson had many problems on his mind, but that he would do the right thing toward Mexico as he was trying to do toward Europe. In the meantime, Gompers reminded Martínez, it was the duty of Mexico to bring her "countless revolutions" to an end. He closed by expressing the great respect he felt for Carranza and the people he represented.[37]

Gompers had by this time concluded that the Carranza

32. Edmundo E. Martínez to Gompers, Aug. 5, 1915; GCB.
33. Gompers to Woodrow Wilson, Aug. 9, 1915; GCB and GM.
34. *Ibid.*
35. *Ibid.*
36. Woodrow Wilson to Gompers, Aug. 11, 1915; State Department Records in the National Archives, hereinafter abbreviated SD-NA.
37. Gompers to Edmundo E. Martínez, Aug. 23, 1915; GM.

government should be recognized by the United States. After discussing the matter with his Executive Council, which authorized him to take appropriate action,[38] he asked President Wilson in a letter dated September 22, 1915, to recognize the Carranza government as the legitimate government of Mexico. In his request Gompers stated that the Mexican Revolution was part of the age-old struggle of mankind for freedom, and time, he continued, had shown that Carranza was the friend of the Mexican working people and the true representative of Mexican democracy.[39] Wilson, in his reply, told Gompers that the Mexican problem was near a solution and that Gompers' views on recognition would affect the final outcome.[40] To what extent Wilson was influenced by Gompers is open to debate, but less than a month later the United States gave *de facto* recognition to the Carranza government.

Recognition of Carranza by the United States is generally believed to have prompted Pancho Villa to order the execution of a number of United States citizens at Santa Ysabel, Sonora, in January 1916, and the same reason is usually given for the raid on Columbus, New Mexico, by alleged *villistas* a few weeks later. Gompers was sufficiently disturbed by these events to consider an interview with Secretary of State Robert Lansing necessary. He felt that a committee appointed by the AFL should be sent to Mexico in an effort to determine the true causes of the border raids,[41] of which there were a number, the one on Columbus being the most important.[42] Friends of the Mexican Revolution in the United States and Mexico feared that war between the United States and Mexico would result from continued border incidents, and they consequently appealed to the AFL to help prevent this trag-

38. *Proceedings*, 34th AFL Conv., pp. 59, 291.
39. Gompers to Woodrow Wilson, Sept. 22, 1915; GM.
40. Woodrow Wilson to Gompers, Sept. 24, 1915; SD-NA.
41. Memorandum by R. Lee Guard, secretary to Gompers, March 24, 1916; GM.
42. R. Lee Guard to Florence C. Thorne, May 27, 1916; GM.

edy.[43] When the punitive expedition under the command of General John Pershing was sent into Mexico soon after the Columbus incident in an effort to end the raids by disrupting the forces of Pancho Villa in Chihuahua, the possibility of a clash between United States and Mexican troops, with a declaration of war following, became greater with every day that passed, and when the clash did occur at Carrizal, Chihuahua, in June 1916, it came as no great surprise. As a result of the clash a number of Americans and Mexicans were killed and wounded and the Mexican federalists captured twenty-two American soldiers, who were held as prisoners of war.[44] At this point it appeared that the wishes of the interventionists for war would be fulfilled, but the labor and revolutionary movements in the United States lost no time in taking steps to prevent a US-Mexican conflict. Among other action taken was a great mass meeting in New York City under the auspices of the Socialist party.[45] At the same time, the American Union Against Militarism called a meeting of three representative Americans and the same number of representative Mexicans to meet in El Paso, Texas, to take steps to prevent war.[46] President Wilson, of course, immediately demanded that Carranza release the prisoners taken at Carrizal.[47] Gompers made an appeal to Carranza to the same effect, and he informed William B. Wilson, the Secretary of Labor, that the AFL would co-operate with the Wilson government in an attempt to maintain amicable relations with Mexico,[48] which was perhaps another way of saying that the AFL would not support the administration if it went to war. Carranza soon publicly an-

43. Anon., "Appeal to U. S. Workers," *International Labor Forum* (Latin-American News Association, New York, 1916); a clipping under "Gompers" in SD-NA. Federación de Sindicatos de Orizaba to Gompers, June 7, 1916; GCB.
44. New York *Call*, July 13, 1916.
45. *Ibid.*, June 24, 1916.
46. *Ibid.*
47. *Ibid.*
48. Gompers to William B. Wilson, June 28, 1916; GCB.

nounced that he would release the prisoners,[49] and he wired Gompers of the steps in this direction that had been taken.[50] Gompers later expressed his appreciation to Carranza for the release of the men, an act, he declared, which had cleared the way for an honorable adjustment of the differences existing between the two countries.[51]

The Carrizal incident was quickly settled, but the circumstances that had brought it to pass resulted in protracted negotiations between the United States and Mexico. It also resulted in a series of meetings by two unofficial groups concerned with US-Mexican relations: the American Federation of Labor and the American Union Against Militarism. Of the latter, it is sufficient to say that it held conferences in New York (instead of El Paso, as had originally been planned) which were attended by representative American and Mexican liberals, including Gerardo Murillo, better known as "Dr. Atl," the revolutionary painter and intellectual who was at this time the editor of Mexico's *Acción Mundial*.[52] Dr. Atl was a friend of John Murray.

A year prior to the Carrizal incident, as we have already noted, Gompers, Iglesias, and Murray had discussed the Mexican problem at length and had decided that meetings should be held between representatives of the Mexican trade-union movement and officials of the American Federation of Labor. Shortly after this decision had been made, Gompers wrote Iglesias, who had in the meantime returned to Puerto Rico, that he had written to the secretary of the Casa del Obrero Mundial, as well as to other leaders of Mexican labor, proposing a conference between United States and Mexican labor which Gompers hoped would soon be held. Responses to his letters, Gompers said, had been most gratifying and

49. New York *Call*, June 29, 1916.
50. Carranza to Gompers, June 29, 1916; GCB.
51. Gompers to Carranza, June 30, 1916; GCB.
52. New York *Call*, July 9, 1916.

he had every hope that the first conference would be followed by others which would include representatives from both North and South America. He told Iglesias in a letter dated June 25, 1915, that a delegate from Puerto Rico should be chosen to attend the first conference, which he expected would be held in the immediate future.[53] For unknown reasons the conference was delayed. A month after this letter Gompers asked Iglesias to prepare a report on Latin-American labor to be presented to the coming annual convention of the AFL. In this report Iglesias was to tell of the gesture which the AFL had already made toward Mexican labor and he was to show the need for closer co-operation between the AFL and Latin-American labor in general. In addition, he was to suggest plans leading to such co-operation.[54]

When the Thirty-fifth Annual Convention of the AFL met in San Francisco in November 1915, Iglesias gave the report on Latin-American labor along the lines that Gompers had suggested. He explained that, first of all, the opening of the Panama Canal had brought the United States closer to Latin America in a commercial sense, and he cited the First Pan-American Financial Conference of May 1915 as an indication of the growing interest of American businessmen and financiers in the possibility of expanded exploitation of the working people of Latin America. Iglesias declared that the union of capital represented by the Pan-American Financial Conference demanded an opposing organization of Pan-American labor to protect labor in the Western Hemisphere. He told of the beginning which had already been made through correspondence with Mexican labor leaders,[55] and he proposed that an AFL conference with representatives of organized labor from Latin America be held in Washington. Countries to be represented at this conference should include Argentina, Brazil, Mexico, Uruguay, Chile, and all other

53. Gompers to Iglesias, June 25, 1915; GCB.
54. Gompers to Iglesias, July 19, 1915; IP.
55. *Proceedings*, 34th AFL Conv., pp. 56-59.

South and Central American republics.[56] His proposal was adopted by the convention.[57]

In the meantime, Iglesias himself had entered into correspondence with Felipe Martínez of the Casa del Obrero Mundial[58] and Joaquín Correa of the Federación de Sindicatos Obreros,[59] and Gompers had kept in touch with Edmundo E. Martínez, whom he had reassured of his support of Carranza.[60] Nevertheless, it was not until more than two months after General Pershing had led the punitive expedition into Mexico that Gompers took action on the AFL-Mexican labor conference.

The decision to call the conference was made in the latter part of May 1916 at a meeting held in Washington and attended by Gompers, Murray, and Judge Charles A. Douglas.[61] Judge Douglas was a well-known Washington attorney who specialized in Latin-American affairs. At the time of this meeting he was Carranza's legal representative in Washington, but during his long career as a Latin-American specialist he represented not only Mexico but Cuba, Nicaragua, and the Republic of Panama as well.[62] Just what prompted Gompers at this particular time to call the conference is not clear, unless it was the growing tension resulting from the critical situation along the border.

Following this meeting, Gompers sent a letter to the Casa del Obrero Mundial in Mexico City which said that the AFL had been receiving confidential reports from a person duly accredited by the Casa del Obrero Mundial and from other sources and that the lessons of the past showed the need for closer understanding between United States and Mexican

56. *Ibid.*, p. 188.
57. *Ibid.*, p. 291.
58. Iglesias to Felipe Martínez, Aug. 4, 1915; IP.
59. Iglesias to Joaquín Correa, Aug. 4, 1915; IP.
60. Gompers to Edmundo E. Martínez, July 5, 1915; GCB.
61. Gompers to Carranza, May 23, 1916; GCB. Frank Duffy, a member of the Executive Council, wrote Gompers a letter protesting the action that he had taken in this matter without consulting the Executive Council. Cf. R. Lee Guard to Gompers, May 29, 1916; GCB.
62. *Who's Who in America: 1930-1931.*

labor. Continuing, Gompers formally called for a meeting of representatives of the American Federation of Labor, the Casa del Obrero Mundial, and as many other organizations of Mexican labor as possible to meet in El Paso, Texas, at a date to be agreed upon. He ended the call with an intimation that peace between the two nations rested in the hands of the wage earners of the United States and Mexico.[63]

This letter to the Casa del Obrero Mundial was widely publicized. Copies were sent to President Carranza,[64] Governor Plutarco Elías Calles of Sonora,[65] Governor Salvador Alvarado of Yucatán,[66] Governor Alvaro Obregón,[67] President Wilson,[68] Dr. Atl,[69] the labor press in the United States, and to various other individuals.[70] Gompers asked each person to whom he sent a copy of the call for his opinion regarding the conference, and he asked those persons who were in a position to do so to give the call the widest publicity possible.

The response to Gompers' proposed conference supported his belief that the time had arrived for a close tie between the AFL and Mexican labor. Dr. Atl wired him that the call had been published in *Acción Mundial* and that the Mexican workers enthusiastically accepted the proposal for a conference as a means of preventing war between the United States and Mexico.[71] The Casa del Obrero Mundial and the Confederación de Sindicatos Obreros in a joint telegram to Gompers said they were appointing delegates to the conference.[72] As no date had yet been set for the conference,

63. Gompers to Casa del Obrero Mundial, May 23, 1916; GCB.
64. Gompers to Carranza, May 23, 1916; GCB.
65. Gompers to Plutarco Elías Calles, May 23, 1916; GCB.
66. Gompers to Salvador Alvarado, May 23, 1916; GCB.
67. Gompers to Alvaro Obregón, May 23, 1916; GCB.
68. R. Lee Guard to Woodrow Wilson, May 25, 1916; GCB.
69. Gompers to Dr. Atl, May 24, 1916; GCB.
70. Copies were sent to Judge Douglas, Governor Ignacio C. Enriques of Chihuahua, and to labor papers including the Phoenix *Labor Journal,* Los Angeles *Labor Press,* San Diego *Labor Leader,* San Francisco *Labor Clarion,* to mention only those in the West.
71. Dr. Atl to Gompers, June 9, 1916; GM.
72. Casa del Obrero Mundial and Confederación de Sindicatos Obreros to

Gompers wired back asking for suggestions as to when the conference should take place.[73] He was told that a date as early as possible was deemed advisable and that June 25 would be suitable.[74] In the meantime, the Mexican delegates proceeded to Eagle Pass, Texas, where they hoped the conference would be held.

While these events were taking place, two delegates from the Yucatán labor movement who were also emissaries of Governor Salvador Alvarado of Yucatán had arrived in Washington. They were Carlos Loveira y Chirinos, the Cuban novelist and revolutionist who had become a member of Alvarado's official family,[75] and Baltazar Pagés, a wandering Spaniard of anarchist tendencies who had been editing *La Voz de la Revolución* in Yucatán, and who was later to work on a number of other radical papers, including *El Gráfico* in New York and *España Nueva* in Havana.[76] They lost no time in conferring with Gompers, who immediately wired Dr. Atl, Alvarado, and other interested persons that Loveira and Pagés supported him in his contention that a date for the conference which would be mutually convenient should be set.[77] Alvarado on the following day wired Gompers from Mérida asking him to set the place and date,[78] but in the meantime a number of Mexican delegates, including Dr. Atl and Luis N. Morones, later the leader of the Confederación Regional Obrera Mexicana, had already arrived in Eagle Pass and were asking for a conference as quickly as possible.[79] The

AFL, June 11, 1916; GCB. R. Lee Guard to Gompers, June 12, 1916; GCB.
73. Gompers to Casa del Obrero Mundial and Confederación de Sindicatos Obreros, June 12, 1916; GCB and GM.
74. R. Lee Guard to Gompers, June 16, 1916; GCB.
75. Gompers to Dr. Atl, June 21, 1916; GCB. Gompers to Frank McCarthy, June 28, 1916; GCB.
76. Gompers to Baltazar Pagés, Sept. 22, 1922; GCB. Gompers to Frank McCarthy, June 28, 1916; GCB.
77. Gompers to Dr. Atl, June 21, 1916; GCB. Gompers to Salvador Alvarado, June 21, 1916; GCB.
78. Salvador Alvarado to Gompers, June 22, 1916; GCB.
79. Dr. Atl to Gompers, June 23, 1916; GCB. Morones to Gompers, June 23, 1916; GCB.

skirmish between members of Pershing's punitive expedition and Mexican federalist troops had occurred at Carrizal only two days before, and Dr. Atl felt there was danger of war.[80] Gompers then wired the delegates that a meeting of the AFL Executive Council which would begin on June 26 and which would last for a week would make it impossible for him to attend a conference in Eagle Pass on June 25. He suggested that if the Mexicans so desired, the conference could be held in Washington.[81] Acting on this suggestion, the Mexican delegates appointed a subdelegation which set out for Washington after they had been informed by Gompers that they should arrive there not later than July 1.[82] The Mexican delegates were anxious to be present during the meeting of the Executive Council so that they could present their program for peace directly to that body.[83]

The subdelegation of Mexican representatives consisted of Luis N. Morones and Salvador González García. Morones, whom we have already introduced as the future leader of the Confederación Regional Obrera Mexicana, popularly known as the CROM, was in 1916 a leader of the Federación de Sindicatos Obreros in Mexico City. In February 1916 he had taken the lead in forming the Confederación de Trabajo de la Región Mexicana, the first attempt at a truly national federation of Mexican labor. This organization, which was formed of representatives of the Casa del Obrero Mundial, branches of the Federación de Sindicatos Obreros, and a number of other labor organizations, had declared itself for "direct action, no politics," [84] somewhat like the Industrial Workers of the World in the United States. González García, the other member of the subdelegation, a revolutionist of some prominence from Yucatán,[85] did not play an important

80. Dr. Atl to Gompers, June 23, 1916; GCB.
81. Gompers to Dr. Atl and Morones, June 24, 1916; GCB.
82. Dr. Atl and Morones to Gompers, June 26, 1916; GCB.
83. Gompers to Dr. Atl and Morones, June 26, 1916; GCB.
84. Alfonso López Aparicio, *El movimiento obrero en México*, p. 159.
85. Gompers to Frank McCarthy, June 28, 1916; GCB.

part in AFL-Mexican labor relations following this meeting.[86] Three other persons participating in the conference with Gompers, Murray, and the AFL Executive Council were Edmundo E. Martínez, Carlos Loveira, and Baltazar Pagés.[87]

On July 3, 1916, the members of the AFL-Mexican labor conference made public their deliberations. The document which they issued may be summarized as follows: Relations between the United States and Mexico should be based on the will of the people of both countries and in accordance with their concept of justice. The masses should have a right to express themselves and by so doing help to determine international affairs. This could be best accomplished through the labor movements of the countries concerned. The present conference was to be followed by another in which both American and Mexican labor were to be more generally represented and in which a beginning would be made toward a federation of Pan-American labor. At the moment, however, the document continues, relations between the United States and Mexico made it advisable to postpone such a conference until the end of the year. In the meantime a joint commission composed of two Mexican and two American labor representatives with authority to call a general conference if need be would remain in Washington. The delegates urged that the United States and Mexican governments appoint a commission of high-minded citizens to consider the problems existing between the two countries and make a recommendation for their solution.[88] Gompers sent letters telling of this conference and copies of its conclusions to both President Wilson[89] and President Carranza,[90] and the full text was

86. Gompers to Dr. Atl, July 20, 1916; GCB. Dr. Atl came to Washington at the same time as Morones and González García, but he did not participate in the labor conference. However, he conferred with Gompers during his stay in the capital. Gompers to Dr. Atl, July 11, 1916; GCB.
87. New York *Call*, July 5, 1916.
88. Declaration of the Executive Council and the Mexican Representatives, July 3, 1916; GCB.
89. Gompers to Woodrow Wilson, July 5, 1916; GCB.
90. Gompers to Carranza, July 5, 1916; GCB.

published in the New York Socialist *Call*.[91] The AFL-Mexican labor conference was the first step toward the formation of the Pan-American Federation of Labor.

91. New York *Call*, July 5, 1916.

## *Two.* The Pan-American Federation of Labor Conference Committee

Immediately following the AFL-Mexican labor conference, Gompers began the formation of the Pan-American Federation of Labor. Progress in this direction was retarded by World War I and it was not until the war was virtually over that the long-anticipated organizing convention took place.

Both Carlos Loveira and Baltazar Pagés had come to the United States from Mexico with commissions from the labor movement of Yucatán to work toward a federation of Pan-American labor.[1] After taking part in the AFL-Mexican labor conference, they prepared for a tour of Central and South America. The object of their tour was to win support for the proposed Pan-American labor organization. In an open letter addressed to the workers of all American nations, Gompers expressed his approval and support of the Loveira-Pagés mission and explained the need for Pan-American labor unity. He called the attention of American labor to the recent commercial excursion of the High Commission of the Pan American Union—a two-month junket headed by Secretary of the Treasury William Gibbs McAdoo which in the spring of 1916 carried its participants to the major coastal cities of Latin-America—as being indicative of the increasing activity of organized capital. He branded the High Commission as being composed of persons who lacked interest in the welfare of humanity. Its members, he declared, were businessmen who were opposed to the common people, and the nature of

1. Gompers to the Members of the Confederación de Sindicatos Obreros de la República Mexicana, July 18, 1916, GCB.

the Pan American Union called for an inter-American labor organization that would be "a ready and fit agency for injecting into international deliberations at opportune times, consideration for human rights, interests, and welfare."[2] The proposed federation being publicized by Loveira and Pagés, he continued, would constitute "a genuine parliament of man, one of the highest purposes to which mankind has aspired."[3]

Tension between the United States and Mexico had eased somewhat in the period following the AFL-Mexican labor conference, and in a few weeks' time the Mexican labor representatives who had been standing by in Washington in the event of a worsening of relations felt that their presence there was no longer required.[4] This easing of tension was largely due to the progress that was being made toward the creation of a United States-Mexican commission to deal with the problem of border raids and the recall of the punitive expedition. In early June 1916 John Murray had urged Gompers to insist that the commission, then only in the discussion stage, should include representatives of organized labor.[5] Acting on Murray's suggestion, Gompers in a letter to Secretary of Labor William B. Wilson which stressed the good relations existing between the AFL and the Mexican labor movement had asked Wilson to urge the President to consider the appointment of a labor representative to the commission.[6] Apparently the President made no reply to this suggestion, for when Gompers received word that Carranza had proposed that United States-Mexican relations be adjusted by mediation,[7] Gompers wrote directly to President Wilson himself reminding him of this request, and he asked that Secretary

2. Gompers to Workers of All American Countries, July 8 [6?], 1916; GCB.
3. *Ibid.*
4. Gompers to Edmundo E. Martínez, July 11, 1916; GCB.
5. John Murray to Gompers, June [?], 1916; GM.
6. Gompers to William B. Wilson, June 10, 1916; GM.
7. Gompers to Edmundo E. Martínez, July 6, 1916; GCB. Edmundo E. Martínez to Gompers, July 12, 1916; GCB.

William B. Wilson be the person appointed to represent labor.[8] President Wilson, who was having some difficulty deciding on the persons to be appointed to the three-man commission, replied that the body would be too small to be representative and therefore could not include a member of organized labor.[9] Somewhat annoyed by this reply, Gompers retorted that in his opinion a commission which was not truly representative should not be empowered to handle the problem. Furthermore, he told the President, the labor movements of the United States and Mexico were the only agencies that stood distinctively for human rights, and for this reason they should be represented on the commission.[10] But he argued in vain, for labor was not given representation on the commission. Nevertheless, he continued his efforts to get a thorough airing of the causes of the border incidents by asking Carranza to allow the commission to make a comprehensive investigation to determine the identity of the persons who were instigating the raids.[11]

The plan of mediation which was finally decided on[12] was in line with the wishes of Gompers and the American labor movement. It provided that first consideration be given to the withdrawal of United States troops from Mexico, that provisions be made for adequate border protection, and that there be an investigation of the interests behind the border raids. In addition, both the United States and Mexican governments agreed that the meetings of the commission would be "wide open."[13] This provision made it possible for Gompers to furnish Secretary of the Interior Franklin K. Lane, the head of the U. S. delegation to the six-man commission which had by this time been appointed,[14] with informa-

8. Gompers to Woodrow Wilson, July 17, 1916; GCB.
9. Gompers to Woodrow Wilson, July 22, 1916; GM.
10. *Ibid.*
11. Gompers to Carranza, July 29, 1916; GCB. Gompers to Woodrow Wilson, July 27, 1916; GCB.
12. New York *Call*, July 29, 1916.
13. Gompers to Carlos Loveira, Aug. 18, 1916; GCB.
14. New York *Call*, Aug. 29, 1916.

tion collected by John Murray which threw suspicion on a prominent Californian associated with Harrison Gray Otis, the notorious antilabor owner of the Los Angeles *Times,* as one of the instigators of the border raids.[15]

The sessions of the United States-Mexican commission began early in September 1916. All efforts of the United States to negotiate an agreement without first consenting to the withdrawal of U. S. troops were futile. The result was a victory for Mexico with not only the abandonment of the punitive expedition but *de jure* recognition of the Carranza government as well. By early February 1917 normal relations had been restored between the two countries.

The failure of Gompers to obtain representation for labor on the United States-Mexican commission emphasized the need for an inter-American labor organization, and at the annual convention of the AFL which was held in November 1916 Gompers did not delay in asking for authority from the convention to create the Pan-American Federation of Labor Conference Committee,[16] the agency that would lay the groundwork for the Pan-American Federation of Labor. His request was granted and a committee of four was named: Samuel Gompers, chairman; John Murray, secretary; Santiago Iglesias, committeeman; and Carlos Loveira, committeeman.[17] The first official act of the Conference Committee, which was the issuing of a manifesto, took place on February 9, 1917, immediately following the recognition of Carranza.

The Pan-American Federation of Labor Conference Committee Manifesto was written in both Spanish and English and was addressed to the workers of Latin America. It first of all requested that the labor movements of Latin America send representatives to Washington to take a seat on the Conference Committee. It then proceeded to outline the need for

15. Gompers to Franklin K. Lane, Aug. 26, 1916; GCB.
16. *American Federationist,* March 1917, p. 196.
17. PAFL Conference Committee Manifesto, Feb. 9, 1917; IP.

and the objectives of the organization toward which the committee was working. It stated in a few words the threat to Latin-American labor from business interests, that is, that capitalists of North America and certain European countries were spending tens of millions of dollars in Latin America on concessions and business properties without taking into consideration the rights of the masses of the people, which were being endangered for decades and perhaps centuries to come by these transactions. The Spanish rendition of this portion of the Manifesto was more strongly worded than was the English; it spoke of the capitalists as acquiring these properties and concessions "legally or illegally."[18] The Manifesto included a belief that had been expressed by Iglesias with reference to the Pan American Union in 1915: "If the employers, the capitalists, of Pan-America thus unite for the protection of their common advantage, it becomes all the more evident that the wage earners of these countries must also unite for their common protection and betterment."[19] The purpose of the Pan-American Federation of Labor, the Manifesto continued, would be—in contrast to the purpose of organized capital—to permeate the Western Hemisphere with a humane influence; and the influence of the Pan-American Federation of Labor would more truly represent the sentiments of the American people than would the influence of the business corporations. It outlined what should be the primary aims of the working people of all countries: higher wages, shorter workdays, safe and sanitary working conditions, better homes, better surroundings, protection of children, prohibition of child labor, right of association, right of free assemblage, right of free speech, right of free press, and the right to strike.[20] Inserted in the body of the Manifesto, but out of context, is the statement: "Above all things, the Pan-American Federation of Labor, should stand as a

18. *Ibid.*          19. *Ibid.*          20. *Ibid.*

guard on watch to protect the Western Hemisphere from being overrun by military domination from any quarter."[21] This ambiguous paragraph no doubt refers to the alleged designs of Germany on Latin America. A note appended to the Manifesto states that although it had been drafted prior to the recent severing of relations between the United States and Germany, now that the break had come there was a greater need than ever before for a spirit of Pan-Americanism and an organization which would give protection and opportunity for the development and maintenance of "the ideals of democracy, justice, and freedom."[22]

Soon after the publication of the Conference Committee's Manifesto, the United States declared war on Germany, and for many months to come Gompers was occupied with problems relating to the war. Widely known as a pacifist until long after the outbreak of war in Europe, he had by the fall of 1916 concluded that Germany must be defeated even if it meant United States participation in the fighting. In line with his changed point of view, he had in October 1916 accepted a position on the Advisory Board of the Council for National Defense.[23] From this time on the Pan-American Federation of Labor and to some extent the American Federation of Labor itself became subordinate to the war.[24] After a year of United States participation in the struggle, Gompers had decided that trade-union action should be taken only after it had been determined that it would in no way hinder the war effort. In a letter to Iglesias he had outlined his views and warned Iglesias that strike action should be taken only when the strike could be justified to the men in the trenches.[25] He now saw the war as part of the working-class movement toward a better life. "The fundamental issues for which we

21. *Ibid.*
22. *Ibid.*
23. Gompers to Newton D. Baker, Oct. 31, 1916; GCB.
24. Gompers to Edmundo E. Martínez, Aug. 25, 1917; GCB.
25. Gompers to Santiago Iglesias, May 11, 1918; GCB.

are contending," he stated, "are those which give opportunity and meaning to the lives of workers. The war is a struggle between the fundamental principles of autocracy and the principles of democracy."[26]

Santiago Iglesias, like Gompers, had pressing duties which made it impossible for him to devote more than a small amount of his time to the Conference Committee. Soon after the meeting of the Conference Committe which issued the Manifesto, he returned to Puerto Rico to lead the great strike of agricultural workers which took place that same year.[27] John Murray and Carlos Loveira remained in Washington, where the Conference Committee had established its headquarters in the AFL building, and during the months that followed they carried on an extensive propaganda campaign by means of correspondence and through the press. Unfortunately, Murray found it necessary to leave for the West in the latter part of the summer of 1917 because of a strike of Mexican miners in Arizona.[28] This left the burden of promoting the PAFL on Loveira, who remained in Washington until the beginning of December.[29]

In the meantime, three more members had been formally added to the Conference Committee. They were Edmundo E. Martínez of Mexico,[30] Antonio Correa of Cuba,[31] and Cardenio González of Chile.[32] The contribution of these men to the routine task of promoting the PAFL was negligible. Martínez was kept occupied with his new duties as Mexican consul in Chicago; Correa was hardly more than a name on the

26. *Ibid.*
27. Iglesias to Loveira, Feb. 24, 1917; IP.
28. Loveira to Murray, May 12, 1917; IP. Leaflet: "A las organizaciones de resistencia de la America Latina que aun no hayan dado contestación a nuestro manifiesto de la 9 de febrero 1917," signed by Gompers and Loveira and dated July 23, 1917; IP. Florence Thorne to Murray, Dec. 6, 1917; IP.
29. Florence Thorne to Murray, Dec. 6, 1917; IP.
30. Gompers to Edmundo E. Martínez, May 8, 1917; GCB.
31. Gompers to Edmundo E. Martínez, Aug. 25, 1917; GCB. *Proceedings*, 37th AFL Conv., p. 64.
32. Loveira to Edmundo E. Martínez, Aug. 4, 1917; IP.

roster; and Cardenio González, although represented by numerous letters in the AFL and PAFL files, does not appear to have so much as attended a meeting of the Conference Committee. This is odd, for González was at that time one of the most important leaders of Chilean labor.[33] He arrived in the United States in late August or in early September 1917[34] and soon found employment in a cement factory in New Jersey.[35] Although he remained in the United States for more than two years,[36] it seems that except for one visit to AFL headquarters in Washington,[37] at which time he no doubt conferred with Gompers, he took no part in the PAFL although his name continued to appear on the official stationery of the Conference Committee as a member of that body. He was in the United States at the time of both the first congress of the PAFL in Laredo and the second in New York, but he did not attend either despite the fact that Chile lacked representation on both occasions.[38]

The propaganda issued by the PAFL Conference Committee included—in addition to the February 9 Manifesto—a pamphlet on the labor movement in the United States, a questionnaire, a second manifesto, and a number of letters to individuals and organizations in Latin America, most of which were written by Loveira.

The pamphlet, *El movimiento obrero de los Estados Unidos,* was the joint work of Loveira and Pagés.[39] It is a brief statement of the aims, ideals, purposes, structure, and gen-

33. Chilean Commercial Bureau, Inc. to *Pan-American Labor Press,* Oct. 14, 1918; IP.
34. Loveira to Cardenio González; Sept. 6, 1917; IP.
35. González to Loveira, Sept. 7, 1917; IP.
36. Gompers to González, Oct. 1, 1919; GCB.
37. Florence Thorne to Murray, Dec. 6, 1917; GCB.
38. Gompers to González, April 23, 1917; GCB. Gompers to González, July 10, 1918; GCB. Gompers to González, April 4, 1918; GCB. Gompers to González, Dec. 5, 1917; GCB. Gonzáles to Loveira, Sept. 17, 1917; IP. González to Loveira, Sept. 13, 1917; IP. Loveira to Gonzáles, Sept. 14, 1917; IP. Loveira to González, Sept. 11, 1917; IP.
39. Clement G. Vincent to Loveira, June 22, 1917; IP. Margarito R. Chagolla to Loveira, May 10, 1917; IP.

eral policy of the American Federation of Labor. The first copies were mailed out the latter part of March 1917.[40] The object of the pamphlet was to stimulate Latin-American trade-union organization according to the Gompers philosophy and to counteract the philosophy of the anarchists and socialists which normally prevailed among Spanish-speaking trade unionists.

The questionnaire contained six questions: 1. What is your opinion regarding the fundamental issues presented in the Manifesto? 2. What influence would this international workers movement have among the workers in your region? 3. What changes or additions would you suggest be made to the issues raised in the Manifesto, and why? 4. When and where should the organizing conference be held, and on what do you base your reason? 5. What should be the subjects dealt with at the conference and what program for the conference would you suggest? 6. Can you send a delegate, alone or in co-operation with other organizations? [41]

The few extant replies to this questionnaire show that there was a considerable difference of opinion on most of the points listed. A union in Havana gave full support to the program as outlined in the Manifesto. It said that the PAFL would help Cuba's trade unions and it suggested that the conference be held the following summer in Havana or Mérida.[42] A union in Yucatán, on the other hand, took a radically different point of view. It said that the proposed organization should be world-wide rather than Pan-American. It believed that such an organization would help the workers, but it said that the basic philosophy behind the movement should include the brotherhood of labor regardless of race or nationality. It felt that the progress of the organization should call

40. Iglesias to Murray, April 11, 1917; IP.
41. Casa del Obrero Mundial in Guadalajara, México, to Comité Proconferencias Interamericanas, April 4, 1917; IP.
42. Unión Internacional de Dependientes de Cuba to Murray and Loveira, April 5, 1917; IP.

for an equal distribution of wealth leading toward eventual communism.[43] More typical of the views expressed was that of the Casa del Obrero Mundial in Guadalajara, Mexico, which called for direct action against capital in the fight of the workers to attain socialization of the means of production.[44] The socialist idea predominated in the replies to the questionnaire. Many Latin Americans believed that Gompers was a socialist, and one person gave his support to the PAFL idea because he was sure that trade unionism would lead eventually to an anarchist society.[45]

The necessity in July of a follow-up to the February 9 Manifesto indicates that the response had not been as great as the Conference Committee had hoped. The follow-up told briefly of the steps that had been taken and stated that the unions of Orizaba, Mexico, and those of Argentina would give their views on the proposed organization after their coming conventions. Like the questionnaire, the follow-up asked the persons addressed to send their views on the PAFL.[46]

In December 1917, Loveira was recalled by General Alvarado. This ended the formal connection of Loveira with the Pan-American Federation of Labor, although he wrote Gompers early in 1918 that he was preparing to leave on a trip through South America which would carry him as far south as Argentina, and that he would take advantage of this opportunity further to publicize the proposed organization.[47]

The departure of Loveira brought work on the Pan-American Federation of Labor to a temporary standstill. Gompers was still occupied with problems relating to the war, Murray was still in the West, and Iglesias was busy with union and

43. Raimundo Arrellano to Murray, June 1, 1917; IP.
44. Casa del Obrero Mundial in Guadalajara, Mexico, to Comité Proconferencias Interamericanas, April 4, 1917; IP.
45. Emilio Farizas to Julián Salinas, May 12, 1917; IP.
46. Leaflet: "A las organizaciones obreras de resistancia de la América Latina que aun no hayan dado contestación a nuestro manifiesto de 9 de febrero 1917"; IP.
47. Gompers to Loveira, April 2, 1918; GCB.

Socialist affairs in Puerto Rico. The war was still dragging along in Europe, and although the fortunes of the Allies had taken a turn for the better, victory was still in the future. South of the Rio Grande, in spite of the incriminating implications of the Zimmermann note of early 1917, Carranza still persisted in maintaining what the United States considered a stubborn neutrality, and there was a strong feeling that Germany had a dangerous foothold in Mexico.

Work on the Pan-American Federation of Labor was suddenly resumed in April 1918 because of Carranza's unchanging position. In mid-April Gompers received from Judge Douglas, who was still representing Carranza in Washington, a written report of a recent interview that he had had with Carranza in Mexico City. This report was apparently not solicited by Gompers and it is not clear whether Douglas made the report on his own initiative or whether he made it in response to a suggestion from some other quarter. At any rate, Douglas reported that on his way to Mexico City he talked with many persons, including friends of Carranza, who were of the opinion that Carranza's attitude toward Germany was too friendly. Among other things, these persons objected to Carranza's recently cabled birthday greetings to Kaiser Wilhelm. Douglas had told Carranza frankly that this had been a grave error, but Carranza had replied that the message had been of a routine nature and had no political significance. Douglas then tried to get Carranza to give this explanation to the press, but Carranza refused. In an effort to get Carranza to abandon his neutral position Douglas told him that if Mexico did not declare herself in favor of the Allies, she would be "attacked by enemies from without and within"; but Carranza replied that while he was not unfriendly to the United States, he felt that neutrality was the best for Mexico. Douglas scoffed at the idea of neutrality; he said that it was a hollow phrase which had lost all meaning, that neutrality in the war no longer existed, and that after the war was over the fact that Mexico had not supported the Allies would make it easy to stir up anti-Mexican sentiment in the United States. He told Carranza that Mexico needed protection for her oil fields and that she needed money to develop the country, both of which she could get if she would throw in her lot with the Allies. Nevertheless, he was unable to move him. The chances of winning Mexico were slim indeed, but Judge Douglas felt that the projected Pan-American Federation of Labor would be welcomed by Carranza, and he suggested that a commission of union men be sent to Mexico by the AFL to explain the benefits of such an organization. He proposed that the points to be discussed by the AFL mission should include border problems, maintenance of United States-Mexican peace, time and place of the Pan-American Federation of Labor conference, and the agenda for the conference.[48]

Acting on the suggestions of Judge Douglas, Gompers immediately took steps to send an AFL commission to Mexico. His first move was to have a meeting on April 16 with General Alvaro Obregón, Carranza's Secretary of War, who was in Washington at that time. The points raised at their meeting are not recorded, but they undoubtedly discussed the proposed AFL mission. Following their meeting Gompers wrote Obregón asking for letters of introduction for John Murray, who was to head the commission, to those friends of Obregón in Mexico who were in sympathy with the AFL-Mexican labor alliance.[49] Obregón sent him several letters of introduction as requested, including one to Carranza and another to Governor Plutarco Elías Calles of Sonora.[50] Gompers wrote President Wilson of the proposed mission and Wilson agreed to the move, although he warned that the mis-

---

48. Report of Judge Douglas, April 16, 1918; GCB.
49. Gompers to Alvaro Obregón, April 17, 1918; GCB.
50. Gompers to Obregón, April 23, 1918; GCB. Gompers to Obregón, May 4, 1918; GCB.

sion must not in any way be officially connected with the United States government.[51]

The AFL commissioners named were John Murray, Santiago Iglesias, and James Lord of the Mining Department of the AFL.[52] They left Washington for Mexico by train on May 14, 1918.[53] The ostensible purpose of the mission was to continue the work that had already been done toward the formation of the Pan-American Federation of Labor; but its real purpose, as a confidential report of the commission later revealed, was to force Carranza, through the Mexican labor movement, to abandon his neutral position in relation to the war. The credentials furnished the commissioners by Gompers as chairman of the PAFL Conference Committee stated that the objects of the mission were:

1. To bring about a better understanding between the workers of the United States and Mexico.

2. To bring about a more reciprocal and cooperative intercourse between the working people of the United States and Mexico.

3. To lay the basis for the mutual acceptance of union cards of the bona fide unions of both countries, subject to the approval of the particular unions involved.

4. To help secure the economic, political, and social improvement of the conditions of the workers of both countries through economic action, and sympathetic and cooperative administration.

5. To establish the permanency of the Pan-American Federation of Labor between the workers of Mexico and the United States, and thus help secure the extension of the Pan-American Federation of Labor to the labor movements of all the Latin-American countries.

51. Gompers to Secretary of State Robert Lansing, May 10, 1918; GM.
52. Credentials for Lord, Murray, and Iglesias addressed "To Whom It May Concern," in English and Spanish, May 11, 1918, signed by Gompers; IP.
53. Gompers to González, May 17, 1918; GCB.

6. To endeavor to have a representative labor man or two from Mexico to visit the convention of the AFL in St. Paul, beginning June 10, 1918.

7. To endeavor by every honorable means and within the limits of the powers of private voluntary associated efforts to secure the cooperation of the governments of Mexico and the United States in firmly establishing the principles of protection of the peoples and the governments of all American countries against sinister influence or power from any other country or group of countries in the war.

8. To safeguard as far as it is possible the principles of autonomous independence and democratic Pan-American countries [*sic*] from open or insidious attempts of autocratic forms of government.

In a word, to bring about mutual good will, cooperation and confidence among the workers, the peoples, and the governments of Pan America.[54]

On May 18 the three commissioners left Nuevo Laredo for Mexico City via Saltillo, the capital of Coahuila. They arrived in Saltillo on the night of May 19. On the following day they met with representatives of the local labor movement and discussed at length the recent convention there of labor representatives from all parts of Mexico which resulted in the formation of the Confederación Regional Obrera Mexicana. They had hoped to confer with Gustavo Espinosa Mireles, the prolabor governor of Coahuila, but as he was ill with a fever they had to content themselves with a conference with his two representatives, Professor José Rodríguez González, speaker of the House of the Coahuila Legislature, and Rafael Quintero, chief of the Department of Public Works of Coahuila, both of whom showed great enthusiasm for the PAFL. After two days in Saltillo, the commissioners resumed their journey and arrived in Mexico City on May 23. They

54. Credentials for Lord, Murray, and Iglesias, May 11, 1918; IP. The wording in paragraph 8 is as it appears in the source cited. It is probably a garbled translation into English of the original credentials in Spanish.

immediately reported to United States Ambassador Henry Prather Fletcher, who took them to visit President Carranza at the Capitol. There in an interview that lasted close to an hour, Iglesias presented the aims of the commission but received little comment from Carranza.[55]

The commissioners were under constant attack by the pro-German press in Mexico City from the moment they crossed the border. Mexico City's *El Demócrata* and its affiliate *El Nacionalista* were especially vicious. *El Demócrata* called them "strike breakers" and warned the Mexican trade unionists to beware of these "betrayers of the labor movement" who had been sent to destroy Mexico.[56] *El Pueblo*, another pro-German paper, declared they were emissaries of the White House; and in an attack on Gompers it carried a front-page article which began: "Samuel Gompers! What insulting ignominy and abjection is represented in that name!"[57]

Two days after their arrival in Mexico City, the commissioners issued in leaflet form an open letter addressed to Francisco Ramírez Plancarte, the secretary-general of the Federación de Sindicatos Obreros del Distrito Federal, which stated the aims of the commission essentially as they had been outlined by Gompers in the credentials of its members.[58] Ramírez Plancarte replied that the members of his organization looked with favor on the idea of the exchange of union cards, and they believed that plans to aid emigrating workers were highly desirable. As for the proposed international conference, he gave it his full support although he thought that the formulation of a definite program for the meeting should be postponed.[59] In a similarly worded document, Luis N.

55. Manuscript, probably by John Murray, entitled "Labor Delegation to Mexico," no date; IP.
56. Quoted in "Labor Delegation to Mexico"; IP.
57. *Ibid.*
58. Leaflets in Spanish and English: *Sr. Francisco Ramírez Plancarte, Srio. Gral. de la Federación de Sindicatos Obreros del D. F.*, signed by Murray, Iglesias, and Lord, May [25?], 1918; IP.
59. *Ibid.*

Morones, the secretary-general of the newly formed Confederación Regional Obrera Mexicana, expressed the same views.[60]

The outcome of the AFL commission's visit to Mexico was a return visit of a Mexican labor commission to the AFL in Washington. When Murray left Mexico City on June 14, 1918[61]—Lord and Iglesias had already returned to attend the annual AFL convention—he was accompanied by Salvador Alvarez, representing the Federación de Sindicatos Obreros del Distrito Federal, and by Luis N. Morones, representing the Confederación Regional Obrera Mexicana.[62] It had been the intention of Alvarez and Morones to attend the AFL convention in St. Paul, but by the time they arrived in Laredo it had become clear that the convention would have ended before they could complete the remainder of the trip to St. Paul. Gompers therefore wired them to proceed to Washington for a conference on June 27.[63] In Washington they held a series of meetings at which Gompers, Murray, Iglesias, and those members of the AFL Executive Council who were in the capital at that time were present. On July 3, the second anniversary of the first AFL-Mexican labor agreement, the conferees issued the following statement: An international conference would be held at Laredo, Texas, beginning November 13, 1918. At this conference the labor movements of the United States and Mexico would be represented. Presidents Wilson and Carranza would be invited to attend the conference, as would the governors of the states along both sides of the border. The questions to be considered would include the formation of the Pan-American Federation of Labor; the establishment of better conditions for interna-

60. *Ibid.*
61. Confidential Report of the AFL Commissioners to Mexico, by Murray, Iglesias, Lord, no date; John Murray Papers, hereinafter abbreviated JMP, in the possession of Mrs. Ethel D. Turner.
62. Gompers to the Commissioners from Mexico: Luis N. Morones and Salvador Alvarez, July 3, 1918; IP and GCB.
63. Gompers to Murray, June 18, 1918; GCB. Gompers to Morones, June 18, 1918; GCB.

tional migratory workers; the improvement of relations between the United States and Mexico; the promotion and protection of the interests and well-being of the people of the two countries; and the cultivation of friendly relations between the labor movements, peoples, and governments of the United States and Mexico. This was to be primarily an AFL-Mexican labor conference, although it would be a step toward the formation of the Pan-American Federation of Labor.[64]

Events moved rapidly following the Morones-Alvarez visit to Washington. The first problem to be considered was that of organizing a propaganda campaign which would include mass meetings, leaflets, and a weekly bilingual newspaper in English and Spanish. The paper would carry items of interest to the working people of Mexico. It would be published in Laredo and from there distributed throughout Mexico and the border area of the United States.[65]

The problem of financing the newspaper—which was to be called *The Pan-American Labor Press: El Obrero Pan-americano*[66]—immediately arose. No help could be expected from the Mexican labor movement, and Gompers would have found it difficult to raise funds for the project through the usual AFL channels.[67] However, the money was finally obtained from the United States government through the American Alliance for Labor and Democracy. This organization had been formed by Gompers less than a month after the United States had entered the war. Its two chief officers, President Samuel Gompers and Secretary Frank Morrison, held

64. Gompers to Commissioners from Mexico: Luis N. Morones and Salvador Alvarez, July 3, 1918; IP and GCB.

65. PAFL Conference Committee leaflet addressed to Los Secretarios de Uniones, Consejos de Trabajadores y Organizaciones Obreras de Pan-América, Sept. 3, 1918; IP.

66. Gompers to William B. Wilson, July 19, 1918; GCB.

67. Leaflet: *American Alliance for Labor and Democracy, appeal for funds,* signed by Gompers, Feb. 1, 1918. A note attached to this leaflet and signed by Gompers says that this appeal netted only $700., "the amount falling far below our expectations"; Records of the Committee on Public Information, National Archives, hereinafter abbreviated CPI-NA.

corresponding offices in the AFL. At first independent of the United States government and locally organized, it later became a virtual division of George Creel's Committee on Public Information and had branches throughout the United States. Its initial aim was to counteract the influence of Morris Hillquit's Socialist antiwar Workingmen's Council in New York. Later, when it had become the AFL's chief instrument for the promotion of patriotic solidarity among America's working people, it entered into conflict with the Industrial Workers of the World and other radical antiwar groups throughout the United States as well.[68] There was a close but unofficial link between the Alliance and the Wilson government. Gompers publicly proclaimed the Alliance "labor's own creation,"[69] but George Creel privately considered it an offspring of the Committee on Public Information.[70] Regardless of its origin, the Alliance was, on a local scale, more closely related to the AFL than to the Creel Committee, for its 164 branches scattered throughout the United States were based on local labor bodies.[71] Its national office, however, was tied to the Creel Committee both financially and through its personnel. Robert Maisel was the director of both the Alliance and the Labor Publications Division of the Committee on Public Information,[72] and Chester M. Wright was the director of the News Department of the Alliance and the publicity director of the Labor Publications Division of the CPI.[73] Maisel, Wright, and apparently the entire national office staff of the Alliance were on the CPI payroll.[74] Both

68. *Proceedings,* 37th AFL Conv., pp. 94-100.
69. Leaflet: *American Alliance for Labor and Democracy, appeal for funds,* signed by Gompers, Feb. 1, 1918; CPI-NA.
70. George Creel to Roger Babson, July 17, 1918; CPI-NA.
71. *Ibid.*
72. James R. Mock and Cedric Larson, *Words That Won the War* (Princeton, 1939), p. 71.
73. Chester M. Wright to Creel, Jan. 9, 1918; CPI-NA. *Report on the Committee on Public Information,* by M. I. 4-5, The Military Intelligence Branch, Executive Division, General Staff, May 1918 (mimeographed); CPI-NA, hereinafter cited as *Report on the CPI* by M. I.
74. Creel to Gompers, July 17, 1918; CPI-NA. Creel to Robert Maisel, July 17, 1918; CPI-NA.

organizations had their headquarters at the same address: 51 Chambers Street, New York City.[75] They were so closely connected that Army Intelligence in its report on the personnel of the Creel Committee speaks of the Alliance as a "division" of the CPI.[76] Furthermore, requisitions for the printing of Alliance literature were made through the CPI, and according to the official report made by Creel at the end of the war, no less than 1,380,612 pieces of propaganda material were printed by the CPI for the "Division of American Alliance for Labor and Democracy."[77] George Creel himself called the Alliance the CPI's "most important body."[78]

The transfer of money from the United States government to the Pan-American Federation of Labor Conference Committee was a complicated affair in which a number of high-ranking officials, including President Wilson, were involved. Once Gompers had decided on the course he was to follow, he called a meeting at which the Confidential Report of the recent AFL commission to Mexico was to be read. To this meeting he invited Secretary of Labor William B. Wilson,[79] CPI Chairman George Creel,[80] and War Labor Policies Board Chairman Felix Frankfurter.[81] The meeting was held at AFL headquarters in Washington on July 17, 1918. Creel had promised to attend, but he found it impossible to do so and sent instead his two assistants, Carl Byoir and Edgar Sisson. William B. Wilson and Felix Frankfurter were present along with Gompers, Frank Morrison, and Chester M. Wright.[82]

75. Letterheads of the Alliance and the CPI Division of Labor Publications carry the same address: 51 Chambers Street.
76. *Report on the CPI*, by M. I.; CPI-NA.
77. *Complete Report of the Chairman of the Committee on Public Information: 1917: 1918: 1919* (Washington, 1920), pp. 17-18.
78. Mock and Larson, *Words That Won the War*, p. 91.
79. Gompers to William B. Wilson, July 13, 1918; GCB.
80. Gompers to Creel, July 11, 1918; CPI-NA. Gompers to Creel, July 13, 1918; CPI-NA and GCB.
81. Gompers to Felix Frankfurter, July 10, 1918; Records of the Department of Labor, National Archives, hereinafter abbreviated DL-NA. Frankfurter to Gompers, July 11, 1918; DL-NA. Gompers to Frankfurter, July 13, 1918; GCB and DL-NA.
82. Gompers to Woodrow Wilson, July 18, 1918; GCB.

The report that they heard was a dramatic version of the account given by the AFL commission on its return from Mexico, part of which we have already discussed. It emphasized the growing influence of Germany in Mexico, the inability of the Mexican branch of the CPI under Robert Murray to reach the Mexican people, the confidence of Ambassador Fletcher in the publicity value of the proposed Pan-American Federation of Labor, and the conviction of the AFL commissioners that only through the Pan-American Federation of Labor could the Mexican masses be taught the truth about the war.[83] The day following the meeting Gompers sent to Woodrow Wilson a copy of the report along with a letter stating that the PAFL should be organized without delay as all present at the meeting had agreed, and that Secretary of Labor Wilson would personally discuss the matter with the President.[84]

Apparently Gompers had planned to have *The Pan-American Labor Press* published by the American Alliance for Labor and Democracy, which would have been financed by the CPI. But on July 17, the same day that the Confidential Report was read at the Washington meeting, Creel wrote Gompers and Maisel that congress had cut the CPI appropriation from $2,098,000 to $1,250,000. This meant that after the end of July 1918 the CPI could no longer give financial aid to the Alliance. However, Creel hoped that Roger Babson, formerly with the CPI but now heading the Information and Education Service of the Department of Labor, would at least take over the payroll and expenses of the Alliance.[85] Fearing that the propaganda campaign for the PAFL would be delayed while arrangements were being made with Babson, Gompers appealed directly to President Wilson for aid. He bolstered his request with a promise to reveal highly secret

83. Confidential Report of the AFL Commission to Mexico; JMP.
84. Gompers to Woodrow Wilson, July 18, 1918; GCB.
85. Creel to Maisel, July 17, 1918; CPI-NA. Creel to Gompers, July 17, 1918; CPI-NA.

information on the Mexican situation in a personal interview. He asked the President for an appointment on either July 29 or July 30.[86]

On July 29 Gompers called at the White House.[87] There he discussed with President Wilson the proposed PAFL. Wilson was willing to finance the "educational and publicity work" associated with the project, but he believed that whatever he did in this respect should be done openly.[88] No decision as to how the President's contribution should be handled was arrived at on this occasion, but on the following day Gompers outlined in a letter to the President a plan whereby funds should be entrusted to a group of three persons named by President Wilson and disbursed through a special committee of the AFL according to the directions of the AFL Executive Council. Gompers further suggested that this arrangement be supervised by some individual appointed by the President and that the AFL publicly acknowledge receipt of the money.[89] President Wilson did not approve of the Gompers plan; he therefore referred it to George Creel with the suggestion that the money be handled through the CPI.[90] Creel agreed with the President and the final decision, which was arrived at on August 6, was that the President's contribution would be made to the CPI, which would pass it on to the Alliance in New York, and the officers of the Alliance would disburse it as needed to the committee operating the *Pan-American Labor Press*.[91] Apparently both Gompers and Wilson had decided against making public the President's connection with the PAFL. Such publicity would have been disastrous, for it would have borne out the charge of the pro-

86. Gompers to Woodrow Wilson, July 19, 1918; Woodrow Wilson Papers, Library of Congress, hereinafter abbreviated WP-LC.
87. Executive Office Diary, 1918; WP-LC.
88. Gompers to Woodrow Wilson, July 30, 1918; CPI-NA and GCB.
89. *Ibid.*
90. Woodrow Wilson to Creel, Aug. 2, 1918; George Creel Papers, Library of Congress, hereinafter abbreviated GCP-LC.
91. Gompers to Creel, Aug. 6, 1918; GCB.

Germans in Mexico that the movement was backed by the United States government.

The Wilson contribution was not immediately forthcoming, but in the meantime headquarters for the *Pan-American Labor Press* were established in San Antonio, Texas, by the Alliance. The paper was officially under the joint editorship of John Murray, Santiago Iglesias, and James Lord. Murray gave full time to his job while Iglesias was in the field at irregular intervals promoting the PAFL through mass meetings. Lord apparently took no part whatsoever in operating the paper. A circulation of fifty thousand copies a week at an estimated cost of $1,255 had been planned. This figure did not include the salaries of the editors, which were to be paid by the AFL.[92] Permission to publish the paper had been duly received from the War Industries Board through the co-operation of its chairman, Bernard Baruch,[93] and a mailing permit had been obtained with the aid of George Creel.[94] On August 28, the day on which the first number of the paper appeared, Wright wired Murray that a clerical error had delayed the transfer of the Wilson contribution;[95] but on the same day Creel's formal request to the President for an allotment of $50,000 "for the use of the American Federation of Labor on the Mexican border" was approved.[96] On September 2 a check for the entire amount was received by the Alliance in New York.[97]

The first issue of the *Pan-American Labor Press* carried an editorial expressing the need of harmonious relations between the United States and Mexico:

> Mexico is our neighbor for all time—for better or for worse. Mexico will either make or unmake the reputation of

92. Gompers to William B. Wilson, July 19, 1918; GCB.
93. War Industries Board to Carl Byoir, Aug. 16, 1918; GCB.
94. Creel to Otto Praeger, Aug. 8, 1918; CPI-NA. Chester M. Wright to Sinclair Snow, Jan. 3, 1959; in the possession of the author.
95. Wright to Murray, Aug. 28, 1918; GCB.
96. Creel to Woodrow Wilson, Aug. 28, 1918; an abstract in WP-LC.
97. Wright to Murray, Sept. 3, 1918; GCB.

the United States for democracy. Mexico will either win the heights of her ideals as expressed in her new constitution or lose all, dragging the United States down with her. Mexico will either open the door for the United States to all Latin America or close it. All Latin America watches the United States through the eyes of Mexico. All Latin America feels the power for good or evil in the United States through the body of Mexico. All Latin America knows that as the United States does to Mexico so will it do to all Latin America.[98]

Headlined topics for this issue included "Mexico and U. S. United by Labor" and "U. S. Jolts Peonage in Alabama." Later issues carried articles on such subjects as "President Wilson Speaks to Labor," "Austrian Employers Against Labor," "Inter-Allied Labor Accepts Terms for Treaty of Peace," "Proclamation by Wilson to Standardize Wages in U. S.," and "United States Steel Corporation Surrenders to Organized Labor."[99] Letters from prominent Mexicans and Americans were given front-page space. News of the prolabor Wilson government was emphasized, but there was no effort to present a flagrantly pro-Allied point of view. The July 3 issue carried proposals by the AFL and CROM of the points to be discussed at the Laredo convention. The AFL agenda included (1) establishment of the PAFL; (2) promotion of better relations between the United States and Mexico; (3) protection of the rights and interests of the peoples of the United States and Mexico; (4) cultivation of friendly relations between the two labor movements, the peoples, and the governments of the United States and Mexico.[100] No mention was made of the exchange of union cards, a point which the Mexican unionists considered of first importance. The agenda

98. *Pan-American Labor Press: El Obrero Panamericano*, Aug. 28, 1918. The AFL-CIO Library in Washington, D. C., has twelve issues of this paper, including the last issue, which contains the proceedings of the First Congress of the PAFL. The Library of the Department of Labor in Washington has a copy of the last issue. Bancroft Library in Berkeley, California, has the third and the last issues.

99. These headlines were chosen at random from various issues of the *Pan-American Labor Press: El Obrero Panamericano*.

100. *Pan-American Labor Press*, July 3, 1918.

proposed by the CROM called for consideration of (1) appointment by the CROM of one or two permanent delegates to organize and watch over the interests of Mexican workers in the United States; (2) appointment of AFL and CROM border representatives to aid migratory workers; (3) allowing full membership in American unions of Mexican workers in the United States; (4) plans for a CROM mission to Central and South America to promote trade unionism; (5) limitations on the activities of the PAFL Conference Committee pending the outcome of the CROM mission; (6) agitation for freedom of labor prisoners in the United States; (7) arrangements for a future AFL-CROM conference. The CROM further proposed that the AFL and the CROM be allowed twenty delegates each to the convention. It also asked, without giving a reason, that the convention be held in Eagle Pass,[101] although Laredo had already been accepted by Morones and Alvarez.

Next in importance to the *Pan-American Labor Press* as a propaganda device were the mass meetings. Iglesias had originally been authorized to make a speaking tour of the United States from New York to California,[102] but the lack of time made such an extensive tour impossible. In New York City, Iglesias spoke first before a trade-union audience at the Labor Temple.[103] Later, after a well-conducted advertising campaign[104] in which he was assisted by the Pan-American Labor Committee of the city of New York and the Alianza Liberal Mexicana, an organization which he had formed for this purpose,[105] he spoke at Harlem Terrace Hall to an

---

101. *Ibid.*
102. Gompers to John A. O'Connell, Aug. 9, 1918; IP.
103. Office of the Secretary, Cigarmakers Local 389, New York, Oct. 4, 1918; Información Oficial Para Publicar; IP.
104. A memorandum: Meeting of the Executive Board of the General Federated Union [New York], Oct. 7, 1918; IP. Leaflet: *Pan-American Labor's Mass Meeting, Harlem Terrace Hall, Oct. 20, [1918]*; IP. Leaflet: *Súplica,* relating to Harlem Terrace Hall meeting, no date; IP. Leaflet: *Grandioso Meeting Obrero Pan-Americano,* no date; IP.
105. Memorandum: Pan-American Labor Committee of the City of New

audience which included Antonio I. Villarreal and General Felipe Angeles, the noted Mexican military leader who had formerly been associated with Pancho Villa.[106] The idea of a Pan-American labor federation and not just a conference of AFL-CROM representatives was presented at this meeting; and the meeting went on record for "an agreement for the mutual acceptance of union cards by the trade unions of Pan-America,"[107] which was a step farther than even the CROM had dared to go, at least publicly.

The work which Iglesias had done with the Pan-American Labor Committee in New York suggested to Chester M. Wright, who was associated with the AFL on a full-time basis and was taking a leading part in the PAFL campaign, that it might be well if non-Mexican supporters of the PAFL were invited to the Laredo Conference.[108] John Murray supported this idea, for he still believed that the convention should be a gathering of representatives from all parts of the Western Hemisphere to organize the Pan-American Federation of Labor, as had been decided on before the United States had entered the war, rather than an expanded AFL-Mexican labor conference as it promised to be. He therefore suggested that cables be sent to the unions in various Latin-American countries asking them to authorize their prolabor countrymen in the United States who were willing to do so to attend the Laredo conference as bona fide representatives of the unions in question.[109] He further proposed that these delegates be sent by Pullman car to Laredo from New York.[110] Apparently the expenses of these special delegates were to be paid either by the AFL or by the PAFL Conference Com-

York; no date; IP. Iglesias to John Alpine, Oct. 25, 1918; IP. Iglesias to Gompers, Dec. 19, 1918; IP.

106. New York *Times*, Oct. 21, 1918.
107. American Alliance for Labor and Democracy press release; Department of Labor Library, Washington, D. C.
108. Wright to Gompers, Oct. 24, 1918; IP.
109. Murray to Wright, Oct. 19, 1918; GM.
110. Wright to Victor E. Arnheim, Oct. 9, 1918; IP.

mittee. Soon after this initial exchange of correspondence, the decision was reached to invite to the conference all citizens from both sides of the Rio Grande who were "supporters of democracy." An invitation in accordance with this decision was issued without delay.[111] The coming conference was to be on a much broader basis than had been decided upon at the recent meeting between the Mexican labor commissioners and the AFL.

111. Leaflet: *Mexican Workers! American Workers! All Citizens! Cooperate for the Advancement of Two Great Democratic Peoples!* [no date]; DL-NA and IP. Leaflet: as above but in Spanish; IP.

# Three. The Founding of the Pan-American Federation of Labor

While final plans for the organizing convention of the Pan-American Federation of Labor were being made, peace negotiations between the Allies and Germany were taking place in Europe, and two days before the Laredo Conference began the Armistice was signed. The end of the war destroyed the secret aim of the organization, that is, the winning of Mexico for the Allies, but it made possible a return to the original goal of a federation of Pan-American labor organizations which would counteract organized capital in the Western Hemisphere. Moreover, peace obviated what could have been a disastrous struggle over the issue of Mexican support of the Allies, as a resolution already drafted and later introduced to the conference indicated.

The delegates assembled in Laredo, Texas, on November 13, 1918. The first day of the convention was devoted to speechmaking and activities of a similar nature. The opening ceremonies took place in the center of the International Bridge which spans the Rio Grande and joins Laredo with Nuevo Laredo. The two delegations marched in order from their respective sides of the border to this point. The American delegation was led by Samuel Gompers accompanied by Secretary of Labor William B. Wilson, the personal representative of President Woodrow Wilson. The Mexican delegation was led by Luis N. Morones accompanied by General Pablo de la Garza, the personal representative of President Venustiano Carranza. After a short speech of welcome by Gompers and appropriate remarks by Morones, Secretary

Wilson, General de la Garza, and Nuevo Laredo's Mayor Francisco Pérez, the delegations, escorted by a United States army band and followed by a long train of labor unions, school children, and a battalion of the Thirty-seventh Infantry, marched to Jarvis Plaza in Laredo, where the leading speeches of the day were made.

Secretary Wilson, speaking in the name of the President of the United States, made the keynote address. He briefly outlined the historical role of organized labor in the United States and by implication upheld the AFL as the model to be followed by trade unionists in Latin America. Secretary Wilson was followed by Ricardo de León, the delegate from Guatemala, who spoke for the organized workers of Central America. De León was followed by Morones, who emphasized that the Mexican delegates to the conference were not there as subordinates to the AFL but as equals. "Let it not be supposed that, lacking respect, we have crossed the boundary line which divides the two countries to render vassalage to a powerful labor organization," he said. "No, that is not our mission. With due regard to the American Federation of Labor, we have come to deal with it as one organization deals with another organization, and to discuss the far-reaching problems that directly affect the workers of Mexico and the workers of the United States."[1] He ended his talk with an appeal for Pan-American working-class solidarity that brought prolonged applause from the audience. Gompers, whose speech followed that of Morones, replied that the AFL had come to the conference not in an aggressive spirit "but with an outstretched hand of fellowship to bind the ties of human sympathy and brotherhood more firmly."[2] He spoke of the conference as one which would deal with broad Pan-American issues rather than narrow United States-Mexican prob-

1. *Pan-American Labor Press*, Dec. 4, 1918, p. 3.
2. *Ibid.*

lems alone. After this address the meeting was adjourned until the afternoon.

The conference reconvened in the Latin-American Club in Laredo, where the remainder of its sessions were held. The first order of business was the appointing by Chairman Gompers of the following Committee on Credentials and Rules: James Lord, John Murray, Santiago Iglesias, Ricardo de León, and Ricardo Treviño. Treviño was a member of the Central Committee of the CROM, and de León was the representative of the Labor Federation of Guatemala.[3] Murray was made chairman of the committee. His report showed that seventy-one accredited delegates were present. Forty-six of these were from the AFL and twenty-one represented various Mexican unions. The labor movements of Guatemala, El Salvador, Costa Rica, and Colombia were represented by one delegate each. The following officers were elected to serve for the duration of the conference: Samuel Gompers, chairman; Luis N. Morones, vice-chairman; John Murray, English-language secretary; and Juan Rico of the Mexico City Linotypists Union, Spanish-language secretary. Gompers then appointed a seven-man resolutions committee: William Green of the AFL, Santiago Iglesias of the AFL, Francisco Marín of the Organized Workers of Colombia, J. M. Tristán of the CROM, Rafael Paris Espinar of the Workers Federation of Costa Rica, Benjamín Huezo of the Workers Confederation of El Salvador, and Cayetano Pérez Ruiz of Mexico, who represented La Esmeralda Workers Union of Ramos Arizpe, Coahuila, and the Industrial Workers of the World of Torreón, Coahuila.[4]

The serious business of the conference began on the third day when William Green, the chairman of the resolutions committee, began his report. The first resolution, which recommended that an educational and organizing group be

3. *Ibid.*          4. *Ibid.*

established in New York under the supervision of the AFL
to work with Latin-American immigrants caused little comment.[5] Resolution 2, however, set in motion a discussion
which lasted until the session adjourned late in the afternoon
and which set the tone for the remainder of the conference.

Resolution 2 was in the form of a joint statement from the
Federación de Sindicatos Obreros del Distrito Federal and the
CROM. It was reported by the resolutions committee in two
parts. The first part was briefly identified and then set aside
until the second part had been disposed of. The second part,
which had been drafted by the CROM and approved by the
Sindicatos, was dealt with paragraph by paragraph. It charged
that Americans in general discriminated against Mexicans, it
attacked the United States border authorities for their harsh
treatment of the Mexicans with whom they officially came in
contact, and it called on the AFL to use its influence to bring
about a more humane attitude of Americans toward Mexicans. This criticism led H. S. McCluskey of the AFL Mine,
Mill, and Smelter Workers to attack immigrant Mexican
workers for their failure to organize or to support the AFL
unions in the places where they worked. Mexican delegates
Ezequiel Salcedo and Francisco A. Moreno agreed in general
with McCluskey's charges, but Juan Rico suggested that the
reason for this was the discrimination against Mexicans prac-
ticed by American workers in the AFL unions. The result of
the discussion was the adoption of proposals which provided
that an AFL-CROM committee investigate the problems of
discrimination and that AFL-CROM representatives be established near the border and ports of embarkation to aid migrating workers.[6]

Up to this point differences of opinion had been reconciled
with little difficulty. However, the report by William Green
of the next proposition in Resolution 2 precipitated a debate
which revealed a fundamental ideological difference between

5. *Ibid.*        6. *Ibid.*

the workers of the United States and those of Mexico. This proposition reads: "That an agreement be reached as to the best way for finding honorable means to exert influence so that justice and protection be imparted to those workingmen who, for various reasons, are deprived of their liberty in the jails of the United States."[7] Gompers immediately demanded clarification of this proposition by asking indirectly for the names of the persons concerned. Morones replied that the names of the persons jailed could not be given, but Gompers refused to accept this answer as final. Rafael Quintero of the Casa del Obrero Mundial then revealed that the prisoners in question were members of the Industrial Workers of the World who had been jailed for opposing the participation of the United States in World War I. This revelation brought vigorous protest from a number of AFL delegates, and especially from Gompers, who had been one of the persons responsible for the jailing of a large number of antiwar radicals. Gompers opposed the proposition in a long speech in which he condemned the IWW as an enemy of trade unionism. Gompers was supported by Charles H. Moyer, a former member of the Industrial Workers of the World who had been tried along with William D. ("Big Bill") Haywood and George Pettibone for the murder of Idaho's ex-Governor Frank Steunenberg in the early days of the Wobbly movement. After Moyer had condemned the proposition and warned the Mexicans to beware of the IWW, the discussion ended in a defeat for the supporters of the measure.[8]

Moyer's speech ended the deliberations until the following day, November 17, when the first part of Resolution 2 was reported by the resolutions committee. This part of the resolution provided that there would be no discussion in the convention of any subject relating to the war or to Mexican neutrality, and that there would be no "meddling" in the domestic affairs of either the United States or Mexico. The

7. *Ibid.*        8. *Ibid.*

Mexican delegates were quite anxious to have the convention adopt this proposition. The resolutions committee, however, declared that the proposition did not relate to labor and therefore could not be treated by the convention. The convention, acting upon the recommendation of the resolutions committee, therefore voted that it be struck from the resolution.[9]

The refusal of the convention to ban consideration of propositions relating to World War I made it possible for Gompers to introduce a resolution which in effect endorsed the entire general peace treaty proposed by President Wilson and gave full approval to organized labor's special peace terms, which are as follows:

> That in law and in practice the principle shall be recognized that the labor of a human being is not a commodity, or article of commerce.

> Industrial servitude shall not exist except as a punishment for crime whereof the party will have been convicted.

> The right of free association, free assemblage, free speech and free press shall not be abridged.

> That the seamen of the merchant marine shall be guaranteed the right to leave their vessels when the same are in safe harbor.

> No article or commodity shall be shipped or delivered in interstate commerce in the production of which children under the age of sixteen years have been employed or permitted to work.

> It shall be declared that the basic workday in industry and commerce shall not exceed eight hours per day.

> Trial by jury shall be established.[10]

John Alpine, a member of the AFL Executive Council, moved that this resolution be adopted, but Morones imme-

9. *Ibid.*    10. *Ibid.*

diately opposed its consideration by the convention because the first part, that relating to the general peace terms, did not concern labor. His objection started a controversy even more stormy than the one over the IWW proposition. Gompers argued that his resolution dealt with a problem that was definitely the concern of labor and cited the fact that his proposals had already been adopted by the labor movements of the United States, Great Britain, France, Belgium, Holland, and the Scandinavian countries at the recent Interallied Labor Conference in London. Reinaldo Cervantes Torres of the Casa del Obrero Mundial supported Morones in his contention that while he as an individual understood and approved of the resolution, he was not authorized to discuss problems of a political nature and for this reason had supported the proposal made by the CROM that would have forbidden consideration of matters not relating to labor. Gompers challenged the Mexican delegation to go on record as opposing the peace terms, and after a long and bitter discussion Morones and his supporters gave the resolution their support subject to ratification by their coworkers in Mexico.[11]

The Gompers resolution on the peace treaty was the last one to be proposed to the conference. The next order of business was to organize the Pan-American Federation of Labor, the chief purpose for which the conference had been held. The following constitution was adopted without opposition:

> Article I—Name. This organization shall be known as the Pan-American Federation of Labor [Confederación Obrera Pan-Americana] and shall consist of delegates from the American Federation of Labor and delegates from representative labor organizations of other Pan-American Republics.
>
> Article II—Objects. 1. The establishment of better conditions for the working peoples who emigrate from one country

11. *Ibid.*

to another. 2. The establishment of better understanding and relationship between the peoples of the Pan-American Republics. 3. To utilize every lawful and honorable means for the protection and the promotion of the rights, the interests and the welfare of the peoples of the Pan-American Republics. 4. To utilize every lawful and honorable means for the purpose of cultivating the most favorable and friendly relations between the labor movements and the peoples of the Pan-American Republics.

Article III—Representation. The basis of representation shall be at least two delegates from each Pan-American Republic, duly elected by the representative labor movement of their countries.

Article IV—Congress. The Congress of the Pan-American Federation of Labor shall meet annually on the second Monday in July at such place as the delegates have selected at the preceding Congress.

Article V—Officers. The officers of the Pan-American Federation of Labor shall consist of a chairman and two secretaries, one of whom shall speak the English language, the other the Spanish language, with headquarters in Washington, D. C.

Compensation of Secretaries. Resolved, that the two secretaries to be elected by this Conference shall receive adequate salaries and are to give their entire time to the work of the Pan-American Federation of Labor.

Term of Officers. Resolved, that the officers of the Pan-American Federation of Labor shall be elected for the term of one year.

Expenses of Federation. Resolved, that the upkeep and expense of the Pan-American Federation of Labor, its officials, headquarters, etc., shall be borne by the Pan-American countries represented on a pro rata basis.

Election of Officials. Resolved, that before this International Labor Conference adjourns, it shall elect the officials herein referred to.[12]

12. *Ibid.*

Shortly before the conference came to a close, the question of the exchange of union cards, which up to this time had not been mentioned, was brought up for discussion by Guillermo Quiroz, the delegate from Local 86 of the AFL Mine, Mill, and Smelters Union. He presented three questions to the chairman of the resolutions committee: "Will the American unions agree to admit Mexican workers into their ranks? Will Mexican members have the same rights and privileges as American members? Will the antagonism of races continue within the organizations?"[13] William Green evaded the first question by saying that each member union of the American Federation of Labor had its own rules for admission. Morones was not satisfied with this reply, for an agreement on the exchange of union cards had been one of the chief reasons why the Mexican trade unionists had supported the idea of a federation of Pan-American labor. He therefore pressed Green for a more satisfactory answer and suggested that it be agreed by the conference that there be a free exchange of union cards without payment of an initiation fee. Gompers ended discussion of the matter by stating that the AFL had no authority to make its unions exchange union cards. Replying to the second question, Green said that the unions affiliated with the AFL did not discriminate against their members because of race, creed, or color. This patently untrue statement was not contested by any of the delegates. As for the third question, Green had no answer other than that the elimination of the prevailing antagonism between Americans and Mexicans was one of the objectives of the PAFL.[14]

The election of officers was accomplished with no difficulty. Gompers was named chairman, John Murray was given the post of English-language secretary and Canuto A. Vargas, an outstanding member of the AFL Mine, Mill, and Smelter Workers Union in Arizona, was elected Spanish-language secretary.[15] Some discussion arose over the place to hold the first

13. *Ibid.*          14. *Ibid.*          15. *Ibid.*

congress, but the conference finally decided to hold it in Panama, beginning July 7, 1919. This place was not entirely satisfactory to some of the Mexican delegates; therefore, at a joint meeting of a group of Mexican representatives and the Executive Council of the AFL, which was held in San Antonio, Texas, a few days after the Laredo Conference had adjourned, this question was again considered. Morones wanted the convention to be held in Havana; but when James Duncan of the AFL Executive Council suggested that New York was more suitable because of its accessibility and because it was a center of information and publicity, it was agreed by all that the next meeting would be held in New York. Approval of this change was later obtained from Ricardo de León, Rafael Paris Espinar, and Benjamín Huezo, the representatives at the Laredo Conference of Guatemala, Costa Rica, and El Salvador respectively.[16] The Laredo Conference was adjourned sine die on November 18, 1918.

Soon after he returned to Washington from the Laredo Conference,[17] Gompers began to make plans for the future congress of the PAFL. His first move was to appoint Santiago Iglesias as the official representative of the AFL to the labor movements of Latin America. In the future Iglesias was not only to continue his work in Puerto Rico as he had in the past, but he was also to perform the following tasks outlined for him by Gompers: help the Latin-American workers along the lines set down at Laredo; get in touch with Latin-American labor leaders either personally or through correspondence; bring about a more reciprocal relation between Latin-American labor and the AFL; dispense information concerning the aceptance of union cards of workers from other countries by the AFL unions; encourage the Latin-Ameri-

16. Minutes of the AFL Executive Council, Nov. 11-12, 1918.
17. At the time it was held, the International Conference at Laredo was called by this name, and the 1919 meeting in New York was referred to as the First Congress. When the latter met it called itself the Second Congress and referred to the Laredo meeting as the First Congress.

can workers to strive for improved social, economic, and political conditions through sympathetic legislation and administration; spread the principles of the Pan-American Federation of Labor throughout Latin America; try to get direct labor representatives sent to the coming PAFL congress; and attempt to obtain the co-operation of Latin-American governments in establishing the principle of allowing the working people in all countries to work out their own salvation.[18] An itinerary for Iglesias was also prepared by Gompers: Iglesias was to leave New York in mid-December for Puerto Rico, where he would remain for not more than two weeks. From Puerto Rico he was to proceed to the Dominican Republic for a week's stay. He would then continue on to Cuba, where he would remain for a week or ten days before returning to New York.[19] Later this itinerary was expanded to include Central America.[20] To expedite his work, Iglesias was given credentials as a newspaper correspondent for the American Alliance for Labor and Democracy.[21]

In February 1919 another step to promote the PAFL was taken. This was the formation in New York of the Auxiliary Committee of the PAFL which had been decided on by the Laredo Conference. Composed of ten members who had been bona fide unionists in their native countries, this committee was to perform three tasks: to correspond with labor leaders in Latin America in an effort to have delegates sent to the coming PAFL congress, to enlarge the committee itself with eligible representatives of Latin-American labor living in New York, and to explain to their countrymen the ideals of organized labor in the United States.[22]

18. Gompers to Iglesias, Nov. 29, 1918; IP.
19. Gompers to Iglesias, Dec. 7, 1918; IP.
20. Gompers to Iglesias, Jan. 8, 1919; GCB.
21. "To Whom It May Concern," signed Frank E. Walsh, editor, News Service Department, American Alliance for Labor and Democracy, Dec. 18, 1918; IP.
22. *Proceedings* of the Second Congress of the Pan-American Federation of Labor, July 7-10, 1919, p. 14; hereinafter abbreviated *Proceedings*, 2nd PAFL Cong.

In the meantime John Murray and Canuto A. Vargas had on January 4, 1919, established permanent headquarters for the PAFL in the American Federation of Labor Building in Washington. Their first report was issued on April 4, 1919. In it they told of a recent appeal which the CROM had made to the PAFL asking for aid in preventing the passage by the Carranza government of legislation which would have crippled the Mexican trade-union movement. Specifically, the aim of Carranza was to alter the Constitution of 1917 so as to give power to the president to declare illegal any strike which in his judgment was detrimental to the public welfare. Murray and Vargas reported that they had given this matter wide publicity in the labor and public press of the United States and Latin America.[23] Furthermore, in a telegram to the Mexican Senate which strongly opposed the proposed legislation, they had declared that a nation deprived of the right to strike was a nation of slaves.[24] A similarly worded telegram was sent to President Carranza.[25]

Except for the abovementioned action, nothing of great consequence was accomplished by the PAFL between the end of the Laredo Conference and the beginning of the Second Congress, as the New York meeting in July 1919 was called. This was due in part to the fact that Gompers was deeply involved in President Wilson's fight for the League of Nations and consequently had little time to spare for matters of less importance. In addition, John Murray's rapidly failing health made it necessary for him to withdraw completely from active work before the Second Congress had convened.

The Second Congress of the PAFL assembled at the Continental Hotel in New York on July 7, 1919. It was a small body compared to the one that had gathered at Laredo. Pres-

---

23. Report of the Secretaries and Treasurer of the Pan-American Federation of Labor for the Three Months Ending April 4, 1919; John Murray Collection, Bancroft Library, Berkeley, California, hereinafter abbreviated JMC.

24. Gompers, Murray, and Vargas to the Secretaries of the Senate of Mexico, April 17, 1919; GCB.

25. *Proceedings*, 2nd PAFL Cong.,p. 12.

ent were twenty-six delegates representing eight nations: the United States, Mexico, Peru, Honduras, Ecuador, El Salvador, Nicaragua, and the Dominican Republic.[26] A delegation from Chile which had already reached Panama was unable to be at the congress because of lack of transportation from Panama to New York.[27]

The first subject discussed at the Second Congress was the controversial resolution adopted at the Laredo Conference which concerned the peace treaty and its associated labor charter. As it was not dealt with in the secretary's report, Mexican Delegate J. de Borrán of the Tampico branch of the Casa del Obrero Mundial asked that the congress be informed of its disposition. Gompers then told of the effort that he and four other members of the Executive Council of the AFL had made to get the labor clauses adopted while on their recent mission to the peace conference in Paris. The peace commissioners had rejected all of the proposals of the PAFL except for the following: the League Covenant, self-determination of nations, and a declaration against child labor. In addition, a clause calling for equal pay for equal work by women, which Gompers himself had introduced, had been accepted by the peace commissioners and made part of the labor charter. Not accepted by the commissioners were the Laredo resolutions that labor is not a commodity; that industrial servitude be forbidden; that seamen be given the right to strike when in safe harbor; that trial by jury be adopted by all countries; and that the principle of freedom of speech, press, and assembly be universally accepted.[28]

Following Gompers' explanation, the AFL introduced a resolution supporting the Treaty of Versailles with its League Covenant, both of which contained clauses providing for the creation of the body which came to be known as the International Labor Organization. The Mexicans were strong supporters of international labor unity, but Morones refused to

26. *Ibid.*, pp. 8-9.     27. *Ibid.*, p. 7.     28. *Ibid.*, pp. 18-19.

support the full resolution and insisted that only that portion which related to labor should be considered by the congress. However, he soon showed his willingness to compromise and support the resolution in its entirety provided that the PAFL go on record as demanding that all countries be eligible for membership in the League of Nations. The resolution was so amended and passed with no further discussion.[29]

Considerable debate arose over a proposal by the AFL that in the future only wage earners would be recognized as delegates to the congresses of the PAFL. This proposal was made after the credentials of two delegates from Ecuador had been questioned by the Credentials Committee. Neither of these delegates was a wage earner, but they had been seated along with several other delegates of the same status. There was a lively discussion of this matter with several Latin-American delegates stoutly maintaining that the question of representation should be decided by the persons being represented in the PAFL and not by the organization itself. Others protested that if intellectuals were not allowed to represent the Latin-American workers, there would be little representation because the workers were not capable of representing themselves. Delegate Gómez Rouhand, a Latin-American intellectual residing in New York but representing the workers of Nicaragua, declared that the future of the trade-union movement in many Latin-American countries lay in the hands of the intellectuals because of the extremely depressed status of the wage earners. But despite all the arguments put forth to the contrary, Gompers refused to give up his contention that the workers of the world must solve their own problems without the aid of the intellectuals. The result was the passage of a resolution providing that in the future all delegates must be wage earners and members of the unions in their respective trades.[30]

A long report on Santo Domingo followed the discussion

29. *Ibid.*, pp. 30-31, 35.          30. *Ibid.*, pp. 32-35.

on representation. It was given by José Eugenio Kunhardt of the Hermandad Comunal Nacionalista of the Dominican Republic. He reviewed the history of his country and showed how it had fallen under the control of the United States during the days of President Theodore Roosevelt and had remained under American domination since that time. He asked the PAFL to help the Dominicans regain their freedom. Without debate the congress voted to have the AFL inquire into the matter and take appropriate action.[31]

Another international problem which the Second Congress was called on to consider was that of Tacna-Arica. Despite the fact that seriously strained relations had existed between Chile and Peru since the War of the Pacific, the labor movements of the two countries had in recent years co-operated to the extent of exchanging fraternal delegates to their labor congresses. However, the expulsion of Peruvians from the Tacna-Arica area by Chile in November 1918 had brought this amicable relationship to an end.[32] The Peruvian delegates to the Second Congress called on the delegates to help solve the Tacna-Arica problem before it resulted in war. Specifically, the Peruvians asked the PAFL to use its influence to have the United States government mediate the dispute. The resolutions committee was of the opinion that it would be best if the congress simply went on record as supporting a solution of the problem while leaving the details of the solution in the hands of the PAFL Executive Committee. The delegates adopted this proposal of the resolutions committee without opposition or debate.[33]

The last issue of importance dealt with by the Second Congress was immigration into the United States. Inasmuch as the basic principle of wage control held by Gompers and the AFL was that higher wages result from a limited labor supply, it was essential to keep immigration at a low level. Even before World War I an alarming number of persons had been

31. *Ibid.,* pp. 37-41.     32. *Ibid.,* p. 14.     33. *Ibid.,* pp. 43-48.

coming to the United States from depressed and backward sections of Europe. Already the government had made some efforts to restrict immigration, but the measures taken were not sufficient to hinder seriously the increased flow immediately following the war. In June 1919 the annual convention of the AFL had adopted a resolution opposing all immigration into the United States for a given number of years. In this resolution the AFL had not excepted Mexico. Morones, who was present at the convention as a fraternal delegate, had felt that the AFL was making a grave mistake,[34] but he later became convinced of the justice of the resolution. Early in the Second Congress both Morones and Mexican Delegate J. de Borrán had broached the subject of immigration.[35] Borrán's object was clearly to embarrass the AFL, while Morones was acting as a peacemaker. Morones had introduced at this time a resolution—which was adopted—requiring that the AFL explain to the congress why it had adopted such a severe anti-immigration measure at its recent convention.[36] For the time being the matter was dropped, but as the congress was nearing its end, Gompers, in an outline history of immigration into the United States, argued the case for the AFL. Morones, in reply, accepted Gompers' explanation and stated that his object in asking for clarification had been primarily to establish the principle that any member union of the PAFL which took action that appeared to be contrary to the spirit or principles of the Laredo Conference would be required to justify its action to the other members of the PAFL.[37] Harmony was thus preserved, but the problems of immigration of Latin Americans into the United States was to rise again in later years to plague the AFL.

The Second Congress set the pattern for succeeding ones.

34. John Reed, "The Convention of the Dead," *Liberator*, Aug. 1919, pp. 12-20.
35. *Proceedings*, 2nd PAFL Cong., pp. 19-20.
36. *Ibid.*, p. 36.
37. *Ibid.*, pp. 54-57.

It revealed a working alliance between Gompers and Morones which was strengthened as time went by. The resolutions adopted by the Second Congress, some thirty in number, reflected the philosophy of Gompers rather than that of any Latin-American labor leader; and after the congress had adjourned, Gompers set to work to carry out as far as possible the resolutions that had been adopted. Among these was one concerning the Pan American Union and its relation to Latin-American labor.

As we have already noted, one of the chief reasons for organizing the PAFL was the belief that the First Pan-American Financial Conference, which was held in 1915 under the auspices of the Pan American Union, presaged a drive of organized capital against unorganized labor in Latin America. Following the First Financial Conference, Gompers made repeated efforts to convince Secretary of the Treasury William Gibbs McAdoo that the AFL should be allowed to take part in those activities of the Pan American Union which related to financial affairs and consequently to human welfare.[38] For the time being he made no impression on McAdoo,[39] but a year later he resumed his campaign. In a long letter to McAdoo he expounded his laissez faire theory of labor-government relations: that labor must be given the opportunity to compete with capital and thus through its own innate economic power determine its own destiny. Gompers was firmly convinced that the greatness of a nation lay not in national wealth in the narrow sense of its having a prosperous capitalist class, but in the broader sense of its having a prosperous population including all classes. Applying his philosophy to Latin America, he declared: "No international agreement between the Pan-American countries will be on a sound basis that does not take into consideration the welfare of the workers of those countries, for the welfare of the workers cannot

---

38. Gompers to William Gibbs McAdoo, June 23, 1915; GM.
39. Gompers to McAdoo, July 2, 1915; GM.

be separated from the best interests of the nation and national progress."[40] What Gompers now wanted was a seat on the projected Second Pan-American Financial Conference, which was to be held in 1917. Six months later, after the United States Congress had voted funds for the conference, he asked for labor representation. Up to this time McAdoo had argued that he had no voice in the appointments, but now Gompers pointed out to him that the wording of the recent appropriations bill authorized him, the Secretary of the Treasury, to invite at his discretion representative citizens of the United States, and to Gompers this meant genuine representatives of the mass of Americans, who were workingmen. He did not consider businessmen to be "representative" citizens. "It is a matter of common information," he wrote McAdoo, "that unfortunately the morality and ideals of good business are not always representative of the best thought of the people of the United States."[41]

At this point World War I intervened and the Second Financial Conference was not held in 1917 as had been planned. After the war had ended it was again considered and finally scheduled for 1920. This date was made public in time for the Second Congress of the PAFL to adopt as its first resolution the demand that the Treasury Department of the United States include labor representation at the Second Financial Conference.[42] Acting on the authority given him by this resolution, Gompers in a letter to Carter Glass, the new Secretary of the Treasury, asked for labor representation.[43] Glass replied that he was planning to add a number of members to the various group committees of the conference and that he would keep Gompers' request in mind.[44] The outcome of this correspondence was that Gompers was given a

40. Gompers to McAdoo, July 11, 1916; GM and GCB.
41. Gompers to McAdoo, Feb. 5, 1917; GM.
42. *Proceedings,* 2nd PAFL Cong., p. 29.
43. Gompers to Carter Glass, Sept. 10, 1919; GCB.
44. Glass to Gompers, Oct. 15, 1919; GCB.

seat on the group committee for Guatemala when the Second Financial Conference met at the Pan American Building in Washington on January 19, 1920. In a short talk which he was allowed to make before the committee for Guatemala, Gompers again emphasized that the progress of a nation must be based on the welfare of its wage earners. Following his talk, he presented to the committee a resolution which if adopted by the Financial Conference would have required that the agenda of the Third Financial Conference include consideration of problems of human welfare and working-class well-being. The committee for Guatemala flatly refused to consider this resolution.[45] Gompers then made an appeal directly to the High Commission of the Pan American Union, but here he was told that as problems of labor and human welfare could not properly be discussed by a financial conference, his resolution could not be considered.[46]

After this rebuff several years elapsed before Gompers again attempted to associate the PAFL with the Pan American Union. His next effort was made in 1923, when he held a series of meetings with Dr. L. S. Rowe, the director-general of the Pan American Union. The first of these meetings was held early in February 1923 and was for the purpose of acquainting Dr. Rowe with the PAFL.[47] The following November Gompers and Rowe had a second conference. On this occasion several other persons were present. Rowe now showed much more interest in the PAFL than he had shown on the previous occasion, and he told the group that he might arrange to have an issue of the *Bulletin* of the Pan American Union devoted exclusively to organized labor.[48]

On November 27, a week after the above conference,

45. Remarks of Samuel Gompers at the Second Pan-American Financial Conference, Washington, Jan. 19-24, 1920; GM.
46. Gompers to Inter-American High Commission, Feb. 10, 1920; GCB.
47. Conference of Samuel Gompers with Dr. L. S. Rowe, Director-General of the Pan American Union, Feb. 1, 1923; GM.
48. Pan-American Federation of Labor and Pan American Union Conference, Nov. 20, 1923; IP.

Gompers and Rowe conferred for a third time. At this meeting the question of organized labor and its relation to the Pan American Union were thoroughly discussed. The meeting was held in Gompers' office and lasted for more than an hour and a half. Present, in addition to Gompers and Rowe, were Vargas, Wright, Matthew Woll of the AFL Executive Council, and W. C. Roberts, private secretary to Gompers. The discussion centered around a committee recently named by the Governing Board of the Pan American Union which was to study "all matters relating to the international organization of labor in the Americas."[49] As this committee was composed of delegates from Bolivia, Nicaragua, Panama, Venezuela, and the Dominican Republic, Gompers protested that it represented countries least advanced in matters of social and labor legislation. He also objected to the exclusion from the committee of the United States and Mexico, the two most advanced countries in the Western Hemisphere in the field of social progress. Dr. Rowe agreed and stated that for this reason the committee would accomplish little. He expressed his belief that a survey of labor such as the committee was to undertake could best be accomplished by the PAFL. Matthew Woll asked Rowe if the PAFL could obtain representation on the committee, but Rowe replied that such a possibility was unlikely. He suggested, however, that the PAFL make an attempt to get its views before the Pan American Union by arranging for a conference with Secretary of State Charles Evans Hughes. Gompers and the other members of his group, fearing that they would meet with a refusal from Hughes, decided to first get the advice of Manuel C. Téllez, the Mexican chargé d'affaires in Washington.[50] On the following day Wright and Vargas called on Téllez. He approved of the idea of PAFL connections with the Pan American Union, although he believed that the leaders of the PAFL considered

49. Minutes of a meeting held in Gompers' office at 11:10 a.m., Nov. 27, 1923; IP.
50. *Ibid.*

the labor committee under discussion as being of greater importance than it was in reality. He explained that the committee was only a perfunctory affair created primarily to comply with a resolution of the last Pan-American Conference.[51] Nevertheless, the PAFL leaders were determined to continue trying for a seat on the labor committee. Gompers mentioned the matter to Hughes when they met at a social affair and arranged to discuss the matter with him at a future meeting,[52] but apparently there was no immediate outcome to these discussions. The following year the Fourth Congress of the PAFL went on record for labor representation not only at the next Pan-American Financial Conference[53] but in the Pan American Union itself,[54] a goal far too ambitious to be realized during this period of conservative Republican ascendancy.

Morones and a number of other Latin-American leaders in the PAFL were anxious for representation in the European trade-union movement as well as in the Pan American Union. For some years prior to World War I there had existed an international labor movement centered in Europe which was called the International Secretariat. The AFL had been affiliated with this organization. During the war it ceased to function, but following the war there was strong sentiment in favor of its reorganization. The Second Congress of the PAFL resolved to take part in this work.[55] Gompers, who had already been commissioned by the AFL to go to Europe for this purpose, was designated by the Second Congress as the PAFL representative to the European labor movement.[56] Immediately following the Second Congress he left for Amsterdam, where he played a part in building the new International Federation of Trade Unions which replaced the old Secretariat.

51. Minutes of the Executive Committee of the PAFL, Dec. 5, 1923; GM.
52. *Ibid.*
53. *Proceedings*, 4th PAFL Cong., p. 125.
54. *Ibid.*, pp. 124-125.
55. *Proceedings*, 2nd PAFL Cong., p. 36.
56. *Ibid.*

But differences soon arose between Gompers and the European leaders of the IFTU, as the new organization came to be known, and the AFL did not affiliate. However, the Argentine Federation of Labor and the International Labor Center of Lima, the latter an affiliate of the PAFL, became members of the IFTU. Once the IFTU had been organized, the Argentine Federation of Labor, which had always looked askance at the PAFL, maintained that the PAFL was no longer necessary.[57] In the meantime the breach between Gompers and the IFTU widened. The chief point of disagreement was over the autonomy of the member unions, but Gompers also condemned the organization for the bureaucratic behavior of its leaders.[58] Many outstanding personalities in the United States labor movement appear to have been favorable to affiliation with the IFTU, and the AFL annual convention of 1921 went on record as favoring conditional affiliation.[59] Just prior to the 1922 congress of the IFTU, its secretary suggested to Gompers that Ricardo Treviño and Alfonso Caso, CROM leaders then in Europe, act as fraternal delegates from the PAFL to the IFTU,[60] but there is nothing in the record to suggest that Gompers accepted this suggestion. Nevertheless, Vargas sent greetings from the PAFL to the IFTU through Treviño that year;[61] and the following year Morones attended the IFTU annual congress, but not as a formal representative of the PAFL.[62] To the end of his life Gompers remained suspicious of the IFTU, although it co-operated freely with him as chairman of the PAFL at the time of the de la Huerta revolt in Mexico, an event which we shall discuss later.

A few months after Gompers had returned from his work

57. *Proceedings,* 3rd PAFL Cong., pp. 23-24.
58. Gompers to J. Oudegeest, Secretary of International Federation of Trade Unions, June 9, 1921; GCB. Gompers to Oudegeest, Sept. 16, 1922; GCB. Gompers to Oudegeest, Feb. 25, 1922; GCB. Gompers to Oudegeest, July 6, 1921; GCB.
59. Gompers to Oudegeest, Feb. 25, 1922; GCB.
60. Beaurivage to Gompers, cablegram, Oct. 12, 1922; IP.
61. Vargas to Ricardo Treviño, Nov. 12, 1922; IP.
62. Vargas to Iglesias, Jan. 5, 1923; IP.

of helping to organize the IFTU, he received word of the death of John Murray in California. Suffering from advanced tuberculosis, Murray had taken his own life when he realized that his role as an active participant in the labor movement had come to an end.[63] His place as English-language secretary of the PAFL was given to Chester M. Wright, the former editor of the New York *Call* whom we have already introduced as a leader of the American Alliance for Labor and Democracy and of George Creel's Committee on Public Information.

63. John Murray MS.

# Four. Activities of the PAFL in Countries Other Than Mexico

The original objective of the founders of the PAFL was a labor federation which would include the principal national labor organizations of all the countries of the Western Hemisphere; but by the time of the Fourth Congress in December 1924 the labor movements of only ten Latin-American countries had affiliated, and these did not include the larger nations of South America. Those nations economically, politically, and geographically closest to the United States tended to affiliate, while those more distant held aloof.

Nicaragua was one of the Latin-American countries most closely linked to the United States during the first part of the twentieth century. Because of its possession of an alternate isthmian canal route which the United States felt it must control—and did come to control following the negotiation of the Bryan-Chamorro Treaty in 1916—Nicaragua early came to be an object of Dollar Diplomacy. As it was primarily an agricultural country, it had a weak labor movement and had not been represented at the Laredo Conference. Nevertheless, it soon realized the value of the PAFL and sent delegates to all of its subsequent congresses except the third. The PAFL was valuable to Nicaragua chiefly as an intermediary through which its liberal and radical elements could obtain the support of the American Federation of Labor on those occasions when they wished to protest to the United States government, although it found the PAFL helpful on other occasions as well.

Nicaragua was represented in the PAFL by the Federación

Obrera Nicaragüense,[1] which in 1919 claimed two thousand members. Its delegate to the Second Congress was Pedro Gómez Rouhand, at that time a resident of New York, but he was replaced in later years by a more legitimate representative of Nicaraguan labor, Salomón de la Selva. De la Selva was more of a revolutionist than a "pure and simple" trade unionist. As a volunteer in the United States Army he had seen service in France during World War I, and his association with Americans had given him an understanding of American ways and a knowledge of the English language which were of great help to him as the foreign representative of Nicaraguan labor.[2]

The first service which the PAFL was called on to render to the Nicaragua labor movement was in connection with the Nicaraguan presidential election of 1920. This election had been discussed the previous year at the Second Congress of the PAFL. At that time Pedro Gómez Rouhand had introduced and obtained the adoption of a resolution calling for an investigation by the PAFL of United States interference in Nicaraguan politics and asking that the PAFL use its influence with the Wilson government to allow a free election to be held in 1920.[3] After the Second Congress had adjourned, this resolution was considered further by the PAFL Executive Committee. It concluded that there were no legitimate grounds on which the United States could properly intervene in the Nicaraguan election and consequently refused to press the issue.[4] Nevertheless, Rouhand continued to demand that the PAFL take action, and in a letter to Gompers a few months before the election he explained that the government of President Emiliano Chamorro then in power would elect its candidates by fraudulent methods as it had in the past, and

---

1. *Proceedings,* 2nd PAFL Cong., p. 59. This organization was also called the Federación de Obreros Nicaragüenses.
2. Memorandum Regarding the Pan-American Federation of Labor Commission to Nicaragua, Aug. 8, 1924; GM.
3. *Proceedings,* 2nd PAFL Cong., pp. 62-63.
4. *Proceedings,* 3rd PAFL Cong., p. 61.

he stated that the declaration of "no preference" made by the Wilson government would in no way solve the problem of ridding Nicaragua of the rule of the Chamorro family. Rouhand was ready to help the State Department bring about an honest election in which the anti-Chamorro forces could participate, and he indicated his willingness to advise the officials of the State Department of the procedure that they should follow. He called on Gompers as the chairman of the PAFL to help the Nicaragua labor movement in its fight to break the hold of the Chamorro family on the Nicaraguan nation.[5] But the decision of Gompers not to interfere remained unchanged, for Rouhand had presented no additional evidence which in the opinion of Gompers would have justified intervention by the Wilson government.[6]

In October 1920 Diego Manuel Chamorro was elected president of Nicaragua as Rouhand had predicted, and, as in the past, he was elected by fraudulent means. The Federación Obrera Nicaragüense therefore asked Gompers to request the U. S. State Department to deny recognition to Chamorro.[7] Gompers informed Secretary of State Bainbridge Colby of the charges made by Rouhand, and he asked Colby for the views of the State Department on the election.[8] He made no mention of Rouhand's request that the Wilson government refuse recognition of Chamorro.

At the Third Congress of the PAFL held in Mexico City from January 10 to 18, 1921, the question of Nicaragua was again dealt with. This time the subject was the influence of the United States in Nicaragua. In a resolution introduced by the delegation from El Salvador, since Nicaragua had no representation at this meeting, the congress called on Gompers to protest against the United States protectorate over Nicaragua and to ask for an end to United States intervention so that the

---

5. Pedro Gómez Rouhand to Gompers, July 24, 1920; GCB.
6. Gompers to Vargas, July 29, 1920; GCB.
7. *Proceedings*, 3rd PAFL Cong., pp. 61-62.
8. Gompers to Bainbridge Colby, Dec. 15, 1920; GCB.

sovereignty of Nicaragua would be restored and the unification of Central America made possible.[9] It appears that no action was taken on this resolution until September 21, 1923, when Gompers expressed the views of the PAFL on Nicaragua in a letter to President Calvin Coolidge. This letter was accompanied by a document from the Federación Obrera Nicaragüense which Gompers said "was pregnant with statements which seem of great importance."[10]

The death in office on October 12, 1923, of President Chamorro ended, at least for the time being, the problem of family control of Nicaragua. Chamorro was succeeded by his vice-president, Bartolomé Martínez, whose views were of a liberal nature.[11] Upon assuming the presidency, Martínez announced that he would bring about legislative and economic changes which would be helpful to the mass of Nicaraguans. The PAFL Executive Committee in a cablegram of congratulations commended him for his liberalism and remarked that it would observe his work with deepest interest.[12]

The accession of Martínez to the presidency of Nicaragua produced a flurry of activity among the leaders of the PAFL. This was the first time in many years that Nicaragua had been ruled by a president who was sufficiently liberal to allow free labor organization and a degree of labor participation in the affairs of the nation. On May 6 Salomón de la Selva arrived in Washington from Mexico with credentials from the Central American Club of Mexico City and from the Confederación Regional Obrera Mexicana. The Central American Club was an organization of what Gompers called "economic exiles," persons who had been forced to emigrate because of lack of employment in their own countries, and it was closely connected with the CROM in an unofficial way.[13]

9. *Proceedings,* 3rd PAFL Cong., pp. 132-133.
10. Gompers to Calvin Coolidge, Sept. 21, 1923; GCB and SD-NA.
11. Gompers to Charles Evans Hughes, Aug. 21, 1924; GCB.
12. PAFL Executive Committee to Bartolomé Martínez, May 3, 1924; GCB.
13. Memorandum Regarding the Pan-American Federation of Labor Commission to Nicaragua, Aug. 8, 1924; GM.

De la Selva apparently had been accompanied to Washington by G. Narciso Aguilar, who was also accredited by the Central American Club, and it appears that the two men had been sent to the United States for the specific purpose of arranging for a PAFL commission to Nicaragua, although the record is not clear on this point.[14] Immediately upon his arrival in Washington, de la Selva met with Gompers and the other members of the PAFL Executive Committee. He reported on the new situation in Nicaragua and asked that the PAFL send a commission there to assist in the country's economic reorganization. After hearing the views of de la Selva, Gompers hastily called another and larger meeting. This meeting was held on the same day and was attended by Gompers, Wright, Vargas, de la Selva, and Hartwell L. Brunson of the AFL Workers' Education Bureau.[15] Aguilar was not present, although it was at his request that Brunson had been invited.[16] Gompers repeated for the benefit of Brunson the essence of the report that de la Selva had made earlier and then asked that Brunson head a commission to Nicaragua. This commission was to consist of Brunson, de la Selva, and Vargas.[17] Brunson, who spoke Spanish fluently and was well acquainted with Latin-American affairs, agreed to go to Nicaragua. Gompers then suggested that while he was en route he should stop over in Cuba to give what aid he could to the labor movement there.[18] Brunson was eventually furnished with credentials authorizing him to confer with and counsel the

14. Minutes of a Conference of Gompers, Wright, Vargas, Salomón de la Selva, and Hartwell L. Brunson, May 6, 1924; GM. Memorandum Regarding the Pan-American Federation of Labor Commission to Nicaragua, Aug. 8, 1924; GM.
15. Minutes of a Conference of Gompers, Wright, Vargas, Salomón de la Selva, and Hartwell L. Brunson, May 6, 1924; GM. Gompers to Charles Evans Hughes, Aug. 21, 1924; GCB.
16. *Ibid.* "To Whom It May Concern" [credentials for Brunson, May 6, 1924]; GCB.
17. *Ibid.* Memorandum Regarding the Pan-American Federation of Labor Commission to Nicaragua, Aug. 8, 1924; GM.
18. Minutes of a Conference of Gompers, Vargas, Salomón de la Selva, and Hartwell L. Brunson, May 6, 1924; GM.

wage earners of not only Nicaragua and Cuba but of all Central America as well.[19] Brunson and de la Selva sailed from New York in early June 1924 and arrived in Panama the latter part of that month. Vargas was unable to accompany them. After conferring with the representatives of organized labor in Panama, they continued their voyage to Corinto, Nicaragua, where they were met by a delegation of trade unionists from Managua. From Corinto they proceeded by rail to León. At every stop the train was met by large groups of workers. At the railway station in León an estimated crowd of a thousand persons had gathered to meet the commissioners. On the evening of their arrival in León they addressed a crowd at an open-air meeting. Following the meeting they attended a formal reception given for them at the Workers Club. After two days in León they continued their journey to Managua. Immediately upon their arrival there they were again given a reception, and following this event they took part in group discussion. The next day they were received at the presidential palace by President Martínez and his cabinet. In the discussion that followed President Martínez agreed that there was great need of reform in Nicaragua, but he was of the opinion that progressive action depended upon the common people and the extent to which they could organize along economic lines. He had inherited a conservative legislature more loyal to the Chamorro family than to the Nicaraguan nation and this made passage of reform legislation virtually impossible. After talking with Martínez, Brunson attended a meeting of the House of Deputies where a bill to reform the election law—which had the support of the Coolidge government—was being considered. This bill was defeated by a vote of 21 to 20. During the week that followed, the commissioners attended a number of meetings, the most successful of which was held in Granada, the stronghold of the Chamorro

19. "To Whom It May Concern" [credentials for Brunson, May 6, 1924]; GCB.

family. After they had traveled widely in Nicaragua and had made a thorough survey of the economic and political situation, they were urged by President Martínez to return to the United States to enlist aid and sympathy among the American people and the Coolidge government for the new regime in Nicaragua.[20] Only a few months remained until the term of Martínez would expire, and it was essential to build up sufficient liberal strength to defeat the Chamorro candidate at the polls on October 5, 1924.

Soon after this conference with President Martínez, Brunson and de la Selva left Nicaragua for the United States. On July 13, only a few days after their departure, there was a great demonstration in Managua protesting the refusal of the Nicaraguan Congress to enact legislation which would make possible a free election. There was grave danger that the people would take matters into their own hands if reforms in the election laws were not made.[21]

Brunson and de la Selva arrived in Washington on July 22, and Brunson made his report to Gompers soon after their arrival.[22] A month later Gompers submitted this report to Secretary of State Charles Evans Hughes along with his own comments on Nicaragua. Pointing out the danger of a civil conflict in Nicaragua, which would of necessity involve the United States, Gompers urged Hughes to suggest to President Martínez that he call for a commission of representatives of Latin-American states to help preserve peace. Gompers was of the opinion that this commission could be composed of representatives of the United States and Mexico should there not be sufficient time to create a commission of representatives of more distant countries.[23]

20. Brunson Report on Nicaragua, July 29, 1924; GM.
21. Gompers to Charles Evans Hughes, Aug. 21, 1924; GCB.
22. *Proceedings*, 4th PAFL Cong., p. 135. Brunson Report on Nicaragua, July 29, 1924; GM.
23. Gompers to Charles Evans Hughes, Aug. 21, 1924; GCB.

During the latter part of August 1924 a series of conferences on Nicaragua were held in Washington. They were attended by the officers of the PAFL, de la Selva, and G. Narciso Aguilar. The result of the conferences was to send a second labor commission to Nicaragua which would advise and otherwise help the Federación Obrera Nicaragüense in the election campaign. Vargas and de la Selva were given this assignment. They left New York on August 28 and arrived on September 8 in León, where the headquarters of the Federación Obrera Nicaragüense were located. From the time of their arrival until after the election they were constantly occupied with meetings and conferences with labor leaders, politicians, newspapermen, and other figures in public life. Their objective was to get one of the candidates to commit himself to a labor program in exchange for labor support. Antilabor Emiliano Chamorro, the candidate of the Conservative party, was so well known for his reactionary views that he was not approached by the labor group. Luis Felipe Corea, the candidate of the Liberal Republicans, was believed to be in the race only to split the vote and thus give the victory to Chamorro; he was therefore not considered as a possible labor candidate. Carlos Solórzano, who had the backing of the prolabor Liberal party and the progressive Conservative Republican party, was by the process of elimination the candidate to be won over to the labor point of view. Although the chief issues in the election were only two, a free election and non-interference by the United States, Vargas and the labor group wanted Solórzano to include in his platform a long list of prolabor items. A committee of three was appointed by the Federación Obrera Nicaragüense to interview Solórzano. It consisted of Tranquilino Sáenz, the president of the Federación Obrera Nicaragüense; Apolino Palazio, the secretary of the organization; and Rubén Valladares S., a member of the Executive Committee of the Federación.

Accompanied by Vargas and de la Selva, the committee presented Solórzano with the points that they wanted him to include in his platform and asked for answers to these points. First of all, he was asked by the committee to liquidate the financial contracts into which Nicaragua had entered in years gone by and which gave United States bankers a strong hold on the economy of the nation; Solórzano replied that national honor called for their fulfilment, although he would do his best to see that other contracts of this nature were not made while he was in office. In answer to the second item, free suffrage—especially for working people—Solórzano said that this would be his first obligation. His comment on the preservation of natural resources was in the same vein, and he accepted the labor planks calling for modernized education, a farm and small business bank, war against monopolies, and the unification of Central America. However, he hedged a trifle on a detailed question concerning workmen's compensation, the right to strike, and the right to organize, by saying that while his program would include protection for the working class, he would always give first consideration to the general welfare. He agreed to support legislation which would lower import duties, provided that it would not violate obligations previously entered into. He was willing to co-operate with other Central American republics in the matter of Central American currency, but he would not bind himself to any other monetary reform. On the question of the prohibition of the manufacture and sale of alcoholic beverages, he declared that while he was a "dry" by conviction, he did not believe that liquor should be a source of revenue for the government; however, he did not commit himself on prohibition. On the thirteenth and last point, which was composed of three items taken from the constitution of the Central American Federation of Labor, he again would not commit himself entirely. The three items were: low-cost housing for workers, military exemption for trade-union members, and May 1 as a national holiday. He failed to give his support to the first two items, but he agreed to support May 1 as a legal holiday provided that it be known as Labor and Arbor Day. The leaders of the Federación were not entirely satisfied with his views; nevertheless, they gave him their support, and with labor backing he and his running mate, Juan Sacasa, won the election.[24]

Even closer to the United States than Nicaragua was the Dominican Republic. The customs receivership established by President Theodore Roosevelt in 1905 and extended by President Wilson in 1916 to a full military occupation posed a serious problem for the PAFL during the Gompers period. All of the complaints of the Dominican Republic during these years were related to military rule. The country had a fairly active labor movement centered on the Hermandad Comunal Nacionalista with a membership of 2,700 in 1919, which was almost 50 per cent greater than that of Nicaragua.[25] Its most active labor leader was José Eugenio Kunhardt, at first an organizer and later the president of the Hermandad.

The Dominican Republic was not represented at the Laredo Conference because of the antilabor attitude of the United States military government ruling the country at that time. The Hermandad received news of the conference through the February 9 Manifesto issued by the PAFL Conference Committee, but it was unable to publicize the meeting because of censorship regulations imposed by the military government. Kunhardt charged that letters coming into and leaving the Dominican Republic were frequently opened by the censor and that newspapers were destroyed when they were critical of, or opposed to, military occupation.[26] On May 7, 1919, Gompers protested this action to Secretary of State

24. *Proceedings*, 4th PAFL Cong., pp. 91-102.
25. *Proceedings*, 2nd PAFL Cong., p. 59.
26. José Eugenio Kunhardt to Gompers, March 15, 1919 [translation]; SD-NA. Gompers to Robert Lansing, May 7, 1919; SD-NA.

Robert Lansing,[27] but there is nothing in the record to show that the State Department took any action to make the censorship less severe.

From July 7 through July 10, 1919, Kunhardt attended the Second Congress of the PAFL in New York as the delegate of the Hermandad Comunal Nacionalista, which was accepted as the bona fide representative of Dominican organized labor. He presented to the congress the following list of grievances against the United States military government in the Dominican Republic: the Dominicans had been denied their political rights since American military rule began in 1915 [*sic*]; freedom of the press had been suppressed by the military government; the Dominican national government had been replaced by order of the United States military commander; meetings of the people had been forbidden; prices had continued to rise while wages had remained stationary or had declined; and the Dominican law forbidding the importation of Haitian labor except under specific conditions had been flouted by the American authorities. Kunhardt made it clear that he was protesting against military rule as it was being conducted and not against the United States or in opposition to the well-meant aims of the Wilson government. He told the congress that he was confident that the United States sincerely wanted to help his country and that during World War I there had been a kind feeling of the Dominicans toward the United States which had in it something of the nature of patriotism. He asked the congress to help bring an end to United States control of the Dominican Republic, and he urged the organization to support the Dominicans in their fight to obtain the same favored treatment in the United States sugar market as was accorded Cuba.[28] His appeal brought from the congress a resolution to make an investiga-

27. Gompers to Robert Lansing, May 7, 1919; SD-NA.
28. *Proceedings*, 2nd PAFL Cong., pp. 37-41.

tion of United States military rule in the Dominican Republic and to take measures to eliminate the abuses listed by Kunhardt.[29]

In October 1919 the Kunhardt resolution on the Dominican Republic was the subject of a discussion at a meeting of the AFL Executive Council. Puerto Rico had made similar requests for help, and the AFL had already authorized a commission composed of Peter J. Brady of the Photoengravers Union and Anthony McAndrew of the Tobacco Workers Union[30] to make an investigation of conditions in that country.[31] The Executive Council now further authorized the commission to Puerto Rico to investigate conditions in the Dominican Republic.[32] As the commissioners delayed their departure for Puerto Rico for some weeks, they had an opportunity before they left to talk to Kunhardt—who came to Washington in November to confer with Gompers—about conditions in the Dominican Republic.[33]

Shortly before Brady and McAndrew left for the West Indies, Gompers sent a long letter to President Wilson explaining the Dominican problem in considerable detail. After outlining the history of the United States customs receivership and the subsequent military government, he laid before Wilson the three basic grievances of the Hermandad Comunal: non-enforcement of the Dominican immigration laws, severe censorship, and unfair actions of the provost marshals. Gompers explained that by Dominican law both Negro and Asiatic laborers were barred from the Dominican Republic except in a declared emergency. This law had been enacted to guard against a large surplus of laborers who were

29. *Ibid.*
30. Gompers to Iglesias, Dec. 16, 1919; GCB.
31. Gompers to Vargas, Oct. 20, 1919; GCB. Minutes of the Executive Council of the American Federation of Labor, Oct. 10, 1919, hereinafter abbreviated AFL Executive Council Minutes; in AFL-CIO files.
32. *Ibid.*
33. Gompers to Anthony McAndrew, Nov. 28, 1919; GCB. Gompers to Peter J. Brady, Nov. 28, 1919; GCB.

willing to work for low wages and thus drive down the income of the Dominicans. The United States military government had been violating this law by allowing the importation of Negro laborers when no emergency existed. Furthermore, the Clyde Steamship Company, which had a virtual monopoly of trade with the Dominican Republic, had developed the practice of bringing its own low-wage stevedores from the Antilles to handle cargo in Dominican ports rather than employing Dominican longshoremen. As for censorship, Gompers continued, the military governor had decreed that any matter for publication which was critical of the United States government or of United States military occupation must pass censorship, and this censorship had been applied not only to publications but to speeches, meetings, and occasions of like nature. In the judicial field, the provost marshals often intervened in decisions of the civil courts and set them aside at will. Gompers concluded with the statement that conditions in the Dominican Republic under the military government did not conform to the principles of modern civilization and that they were not compatible with the doctrine that "men are born free and must be accorded the opportunity for life, liberty, and the pursuit of happiness."[34] Wilson himself did not answer this letter, but a month later Gompers received a reply signed by Secretary of State Lansing, who reported that new regulations recently put into effect by the military government in the Dominican Republic had practically abolished censorship. Furthermore, Lansing wrote, the American minister to the Dominican Republic would be in Washington in a matter of days and the other complaints which had been made by the Hermandad would be discussed with him.[35]

On January 27, 1920, Brady and McAndrew arrived in Santo Domingo, the capital of the Dominican Republic, after their investigation in Puerto Rico. They proceeded imme-

34. Gompers to Woodrow Wilson, Nov. 29, 1919; GCB.
35. Robert Lansing to Gompers, Dec. 31, 1919; GCB.

diately to investigate the charges made by Kunhardt at the Second Congress. In the course of their investigation they traveled extensively and interviewed many persons of importance, including Admiral Thomas Snowden, the United States military governor. They found that wages for the common people were from thirty to fifty cents a day, and they concluded that this condition was due to the importation of contract labor from Haiti and the British West Indies for work in the Dominican sugar industry. Skilled workers were paid from one to three dollars for a ten-hour day. They were organized to some degree, but their unions were not recognized by the employers.[36] As for censorship, this had ended on January 16, less than two weeks before the commissioners had arrived.[37] After they had finished their investigation, they made a report which included no less than thirty-five proposals to better the lot of the common people of the Dominican Republic. These proposals embraced measures relating to education, hours of work, sanitation, and all the other features of a modern progressive government. Admiral Snowden considered them one by one and commented on what had been done in the past and what could be done in the future to make them a reality.[38]

Not long after Brady and McAndrew had returned to Washington, a conference on the Dominican Republic was held at AFL headquarters. Present were Gompers, Brady, Secretary of the Navy Josephus Daniels, and Tulio M. Cestero, a representative of the Dominican labor movement. It appears that this meeting was held for the express purpose of allowing Cestero to present the views of the Dominican workers regarding American military rule directly to Secretary Daniels, the immediate superior of the military com-

36. Brady-McAndrew Report on the Dominican Republic; in *Proceedings,* 3rd PAFL Cong., pp. 31-55.
37. Lansing to Gompers, Jan. 31, 1920; in *Proceedings,* 3rd PAFL Cong., p. 36.
38. Brady-McAndrew Report on the Dominican Republic; in *Proceedings,* 3rd PAFL Cong., pp. 31.55.

mander in the Dominican Republic. Cestero spoke briefly of the situation in his country and commented on several memorandums containing proposals to restore Dominican independence which had been sent to the State Department in the past by the Dominican labor movement. These proposals were: abolition of censorship and provost marshal rule, and the naming of a commission of Dominicans to draft reforms in the laws. Cestero told how a consultative commission had been named by Admiral Snowden the preceding November, but it had been disclaimed by the Admiral in January because of its views in favor of reform of the censorship and the curtailment of the activities of the provost marshals. The Dominicans wanted a consultative commission with powers comparable to those held by a similar commission in Cuba during the period of United States occupation from 1906 to 1909. Cestero listed a number of needed reforms which included an improved electoral law which would allow greater freedom of suffrage; legislation to democratize the political parties and eliminate party bureaucracies; a guarantee of greater autonomy for the municipalities; a law which would give more autonomy to the provinces; a reduction in the number of provinces; passage of Civil Service legislation; and the establishment of several government services in the fields of education, sanitation and communication.[39]

Some months following this meeting, on December 25, 1920, Admiral Snowden proclaimed the intention of the United States government to bring the military occupation of the Dominican Republic to an end. This would be accomplished by the appointment of a Dominican citizens' committee which would draft amendments to the constitution and make a general revision of the laws of the nation. After this work had been completed, a constitutional convention would be called to consider the proposed changes, all of which

39. Tulio M. Cestero to Gompers, April 1920; GCB.

would be subject to the approval of the military governor.[40] Although this plan would not immediately restore the sovereignty of the Dominican Republic, Gompers was confident that it was a step in the right direction.[41]

The Hermandad Comunal was not at all pleased with the plan for restoration of Dominican sovereignty as contained in the Snowden Proclamation. It would be satisfied only with immediate and complete withdrawal of the United States and an end to military government. The result was that when the Third Congress of the PAFL met in January 1921, only a few weeks following the Snowden Proclamation, Kunhardt proposed a resolution demanding that the United States withdraw from the Dominican Republic without further delay. The congress adopted his resolution and approved a telegram from Gompers to President Wilson embodying this demand.[42] Wilson was shocked and annoyed by this action. In a letter to acting Secretary of State Norman H. Davis asking for advice on this "extraordinary message," he remarked that the AFL was apparently as willing to rule the world as were the Soviets.[43] Davis hastened to assure the President that the newspapers had stated that Gompers had not consented to the transmission of this telegram; therefore it must have been sent by some of the delegates without the knowledge of Gompers. Davis added that Gompers was well acquainted with the views of the President on the Dominican problem, for he had been briefed by the State Department before he had left for the Third Congress.[44]

The fight for the restoration of Dominican sovereignty continued following the Third Congress, and finally, in 1924, United States occupation of the Dominican Republic came

40. *Proceedings*, 3rd PAFL Cong., pp. 54-55.
41. Gompers to Vargas, Dec. 27, 1920; GCB.
42. Gompers to Woodrow Wilson, Jan. 17, 1921; GCB, SD-NA, and *Proceedings*, 3rd PAFL Cong., p. 92.
43. Woodrow Wilson to Norman H. Davis, Jan. 20, 1921; SD-NA.
44. Norman H. Davis to Woodrow Wilson, Jan. 21, 1921; SD-NA.

to an end. Just what influence the PAFL had in this case is debatable, but it is highly probable that both President Wilson and Secretary Daniels were strongly influenced by the pressure put on them by the labor groups. However, withdrawal of the United States did not solve the economic and political problems of the Dominicans as Gompers and the leaders in the PAFL had hoped.

On their way to Santo Domingo, Brady and McAndrew had stopped over on the neighboring island of Puerto Rico for an investigation similar to the one that they made in the Dominican Republic. The Puerto Rican trade-union movement was much stronger than that of the Dominican Republic, but the two countries had similar economic and political problems. The leading labor organization in Puerto Rico was the Federación Libre de los Trabajadores with a membership in the early part of the 1920's of about twenty-five thousand persons. It was under the leadership of Santiago Iglesias, who was also the leader of Puerto Rico's Socialist party. The Federación Libre was affiliated with the AFL, and for this reason its status within the PAFL was for some years undecided. Puerto Rican labor had not been formally represented at either the Laredo Conference or the Second Congress, although Iglesias had been present on both occasions. At the Third Congress Iglesias had been seated without comment as the delegate of the Federación Libre.[45] At the Fourth Congress he was seated as a delegate with voice and vote upon the motion of Ricardo Treviño of the CROM, who compared the status of Puerto Rican labor in the PAFL to that of a British dominion in the League of Nations.[46] At the Fifth Congress, held in 1927, the PAFL finally recognized the autonomy of the Federación Libre when it accepted it as the bona fide labor movement of Puerto Rico and seated its three-

45. *Proceedings,* 3rd PAFL Cong., p. 13.
46. *Proceedings,* 4th PAFL Cong., pp. 8-9.

man delegation, headed by Iglesias, with no opposition.[47] In addition, the Fifth Congress for the first time in the history of the PAFL adopted resolutions relating to Puerto Rico.[48] During the lifetime of Gompers the problems of the Puerto Rican workers were not discussed by the PAFL. The Brady-McAndrew mission to Puerto Rico had been authorized by both the 1918 and the 1919 annual conventions of the AFL, but it had not been discussed at any of the PAFL congresses. The report of the Brady-McAndrew Puerto Rican mission is of great interest, but as the project was not carried out under the auspices of the PAFL it will not be treated here.[49]

The trade-union movement of the Republic of Panama, unlike that of Puerto Rico, was of major concern to the PAFL primarily because of the proximity of thousands of unemployed Panamanian workers to the Panama Canal. The great majority of workers in the Republic of Panama were unorganized, although there was the beginning of a labor movement in the Federación Obrera de la República de Panamá. This organization was recognized by the PAFL as the bona fide national labor organization of Panama, but it played no part in the PAFL until the Fourth Congress.

The most important labor problem in Panama was that of obtaining employment on the Canal. This problem was aggravated by the attitude of the American workers in the area, who regarded the Panamanians as inferior because of their race and because they were apparently willing to work for lower wages and longer hours than the Americans. The Americans in the Canal Zone were mostly skilled workers and members of unions which were affiliated with the AFL. They worked an eight-hour day and were paid in gold. During the

47. *Proceedings*, 5th PAFL Cong., p. 19.
48. *Ibid.*, p. 106.
49. Peter J. Brady and Anthony McAndrew, "Puerto Rico Obrero ante el Pueblo y Gobierno Americano," *Justicia*, año VII, No. 220, 21 de junio, 1920, pp. 12-17. This is the complete text in Spanish of the Brady-McAndrew report on Puerto Rico.

period when the Canal had been under construction, special legislation had made it possible to import large numbers of unskilled workers from Puerto Rico, Jamaica, and the Virgin Islands. Many—if not most—of these imported laborers were Negroes. They were required to work in excess of eight hours a day, they were paid only about half the hourly wage paid to the Americans, and they were paid in silver. In the course of time many of them became skilled workmen, and circumstances forced them to perform the same skilled operations as the Americans for half the hourly wage. Seeing the advantages of union organization to the Americans, they began to seek admission to the AFL local unions in the Canal Zone, but they were not admitted. They then organized their own locals and applied for charters from the various AFL international unions in their trades, but again they met with refusal.[50] Something had to be done to satisfy those Panamanians who wanted to be affiliated with the AFL. The result was that Gompers asked the leaders of the Latin-American unions in Panama and the Canal Zone to consider sending delegates to Washington on or about March 7, 1921, to discuss with the leaders of the international unions having locals in the Canal Zone the problem of organization and to attempt to reconcile some of the differences existing between the Americans and the Panamanians.[51]

Whether or not the Panamanians sent a delegation to Washington is not clear. However, there was a meeting of top officials of the AFL in Washington on March 2, 3, and 4, 1921, at which the Panama problem was thoroughly debated. It dealt specifically with the formal application of a labor organization called the Bureau de Panamá in Balboa Heights for affiliation with the AFL. This application was rejected on the grounds that the members of the organization were not and did not intend to become American citizens, that for

50. AFL Executive Council Minutes, March 1, 1921.
51. *Proceedings,* 3rd PAFL Cong., p. 22.

security reasons the canal should be manned only by Americans, and that the members of the bureau clearly intended to continue working on the Silver Roll.[52]

Grievances of the AFL members in the Canal Zone against the United States government made it necessary for Gompers to make a personal survey of the area in January 1924. He took advantage of this opportunity to talk to a group of organized Panamanian workers regarding their problems. He and his party, consisting of his secretary W. C. Roberts and six representatives of the AFL, arrived in Cristóbal on December 31, 1923.[53] While in this area Gompers conferred with representatives of the United States government, American employers in the Canal Zone, the government of the Republic of Panama, the Rotary Club, and the Federación Obrera de la República de Panamá. In an address to the Federación Obrera he urged the Panamanians to organize and to depend upon economic rather than political organization for a better future. He made no direct reference in his public statements to the problem of employment on the Canal other than to say that if the Panamanians or other non-Americans were to be employed on the Canal they should be paid more than they were currently receiving so that they could maintain themselves and their families "in some decent respect."[54] In a letter to the Governor of the Panama Canal signed by Gompers and the members of his party, reference was made in passing to the low wages paid the aliens employed on the Canal,[55] but if any attempt was made by Gompers at this time

52. AFL Executive Council Minutes, March 4, 1921. Those workers who were paid in gold were said to be on the Gold Roll; those who received their pay in silver were said to be on the Silver Roll. In addition to the economic disadvantage suffered by the workers on the Silver Roll, persons in that category were considered to be socially inferior to those on the Gold Roll.
53. Conferences Held by President Gompers in Connection with Panama Canal Zone Trip, Dec. 24, 1923-Jan. 12, 1924; GM.
54. Address of President Gompers at the Convention of the Panama Federation of Labor in Panama City, Jan. 6, 1924; GM.
55. Gompers and Members of the Panama Labor Commission to Jay J. Morrow, Governor of the Panama Canal, Jan. 7, 1924; GM.

to solve the Panamanian problem it was done privately and was not recorded. In refusing to take more decisive action he no doubt alienated the Panamanians, but at the same time he was acting in accordance with his basic philosophy that the workers must help themselves rather than rely on aid from others. His treatment of working people, regardless of their nationality, was never paternalistic.

With the exception of the countries just dealt with, the PAFL had remarkably few opportunities to aid the labor movements of Central America and the Caribbean. This was largely due to the fact that except for Cuba the labor movements in this area were weak. Cuba had a relatively strong trade-union movement but it was not unified on a national scale, although Cuba had been one of the countries considered most important by Gompers long before the PAFL had come into being.[56] At one time both Gompers and Iglesias had believed that Iglesias should leave Puerto Rico permanently to concentrate on Cuba. This idea was abandoned because of World War I,[57] but it is interesting to speculate on what effect such action would have had on United States–Cuban relations by the 1960's. Iglesias had corresponded with Gompers on the subject of Cuba as early as 1910, when he had sent Gompers a report prepared by representative labor leaders of Cuba. This report revealed that the chief difficulty in forming a national organization of labor was related to the fight between the different political theorists of the Left as to the proper approach to the working-class problem— whether it should be considered from the point of view of the anarchists, the syndicalists, the socialists, or the trade unionists. Many Cubans were willing to follow the AFL in both philosophy and organizational form, but the idea of political action advocated by Spanish theorists predominated,

56. Gompers to Iglesias, March 4, 1914; GCB. Gompers to Iglesias, Oct. 28, 1915; IP. Gompers to Iglesias, Sept. 17, 1914; IP. Iglesias to Gompers, March 24, 1914; IP.
57. Gompers to Iglesias, Sept. 17, 1914; IP.

and unification was not accomplished.[58] The result was that during the Gompers period Cuban labor did not participate in the activities of the PAFL.

Slightly more than a year before the death of Gompers, the officers of the PAFL—and perhaps the State Department itself—showed great interest in using their organization in Cuba somewhat as it had been used in Mexico at the time of its formation. In late October 1923 one Colonel Ahearn,[59] a close friend of General Enoch H. Crowder, the ambassador of the United States to Cuba at that time, called on Arthur Holder of the AFL Machinists Union in Washington for information on the PAFL. Holder suggested that Ahearn confer with Vargas and Iglesias. Shortly thereafter, on November 5, Ahearn had a conference with Vargas and Iglesias in Holder's office. Current problems in Cuba and the work of the PAFL, especially in relation to Mexico, were discussed. Ahearn was deeply impressed with the accomplishments of the PAFL, and he agreed to a proposal made by Vargas and Iglesias that a meeting between Crowder and Gompers should be arranged to discuss the matter further.[60]

Two days after the meeting of Ahearn with Vargas and Iglesias, the PAFL Executive Committee met to discuss the coming meeting with General Crowder. Iglesias was of the opinion that Crowder's interest in the PAFL—for it was clear that Ahearn was secretly representing Crowder—suggested the possibility of a mission to Cuba somewhat like the one that had been sent to Mexico in 1918 when the PAFL was formed. The object of this commission would be to make a survey of labor conditions in Cuba, to promote the consolida-

58. Iglesias to Gompers, March 24, 1914; IP.
59. Pan-American Federation of Labor Executive Committee Conference Report, Nov. 7, 1923; IP. Pan-American Federation of Labor Executive Committee Conference Report, Nov. 10, 1923; IP. Gompers to General Enoch H. Crowder, March 21, 1924; GM. The full name of Ahearn does not appear in any of these documents. He is referred to on various occasions as Captain Ahearn, Major Ahearn, and Colonel Ahearn.
60. Pan-American Federation of Labor Executive Committee Conference Report, Nov. 7, 1923; IP.

tion of Cuban labor into a national labor federation, and to work for the affiliation of this federation to the PAFL.[61]

The meeting of Gompers and Crowder was held in Gompers' office at AFL headquarters on November 10, 1923. Present in addition to Gompers and Crowder were Wright, Vargas, Iglesias, Ahearn, and W. C. Roberts. Gompers, Wright, Vargas, and Iglesias all spoke briefly on various features and activities of the PAFL with emphasis on the role that it had played in United States–Mexican relations. Gompers also told of current labor problems in Cuba and how lack of unity was injuring working-class Cubans. General Crowder then talked at length of the difficulties that he had encountered in Cuba under President Alfredo Zayas both as an informal adviser to the Cuban president and as ambassador. He had in the beginning been able to persuade Zayas to inaugurate a reform program which was designed primarily to eliminate graft and corruption in the government. He had proposed, and Zayas had agreed, to replace seven of the nine members of the Zayas cabinet, to reform the lottery law, and to make a number of other major reforms. In return for these changes, a fifty-million-dollar loan for Cuba was floated in the United States. After Zayas had made some of the changes mentioned the loan was negotiated, but Zayas then dismissed the seven new members of his cabinet who had been approved by Crowder, enacted a more offensive lottery law than the one that had been repealed, and took similar action in regard to other reforms. The result of Zayas' duplicity was that Crowder felt conventional political means had failed in Cuba and other means would have to be adopted to bring about the reforms needed. He then spoke on Cuban labor and presented a point of view that coincided with that of the officers of the PAFL. He agreed that a survey of Cuban labor matters must be made and he concurred in a suggestion that a PAFL mission be sent to Cuba to make this survey and to

61. *Ibid.*

invite the leaders of the Cuban labor movement to the next congress of the PAFL. After he had finished speaking, the meeting was adjourned to meet again on November 13.[62] Hardly more than an hour after adjournment General Crowder returned alone to Gompers' office. He and Gompers talked privately for some time. No record was kept of their discussion other than that it took place.[63]

It is highly probable that General Crowder in his private conversation with Gompers decided to drop the matter of direct PAFL aid, for it appears that the November 13 meeting was never held. On March 21, 1924, Gompers in a letter to Crowder expressed hope that he could visit Cuba while Crowder was still in office there, but he made no reference to the meetings in Washington.[64] As far as the record is concerned, this was the end of the matter, although Cuban labor did unify to some extent in the years just ahead, and the PAFL began to play an important part in Cuban affairs.

While Gompers and the PAFL were considering action in relation to Cuba, they also became involved in a feud with President Juan Vicente Gómez of Venezuela. The first action against Gómez was taken by the Third Congress of the PAFL in 1921, when the Mexican delegation introduced a resolution condemning the tyranny existing in Venezuela and asking that an investigation of conditions there be made and that steps be taken to aid the Venezuelan working class against the dictator. There was some objection to this measure. It was especially opposed by Victor M. de Castro, a delegate from the Dominican Republic, on the ground that it related to the domestic affairs of a nation and therefore could not properly be discussed by the congress, but he was opposed by José Eugenio Kunhardt and Rafael Estrella Ureña, the two other

62. Pan-American Federation of Labor Executive Committee Conference Report, Nov. 10, 1923; IP.

63. A memorandum dated Nov. 10, 1923, containing this information and nothing else; IP.

64. Gompers to General Enoch H. Crowder, March 21, 1924; GM.

delegates from the Dominican Republic. After some further discussion the resolution was adopted.[65]

Following the example of the PAFL, the Portland convention of the American Federation of Labor in October 1923 took similar action in regard to Gómez, although its resolution was in a somewhat milder tone. In a resolution introduced by delegate Luis Muñoz Marín of Puerto Rico, the AFL declared that for ten years it had been alleged that the Gómez government had kept itself in power by violence and tyrannous oppression, that it had destroyed the right of free suffrage, the right of free speech, the right of assembly, the right of organization, and the right to strike. Furthermore, the resolution continued, it had been alleged that the methods used by the Gómez government to stifle protest were equal to those used during the darkest period of the history of mankind, for they included confinement without trial in vermin-infested dungeons, shackling with ball and chain, stretching on the rack, and hanging by the toes, fingers, and unmentionable parts of the body. The resolution denounced any kind of despotism in Venezuela or in any other country. It called on the PAFL to investigate these allegations; should they be proved, the AFL would ask the United States government to break diplomatic relations with Venezuela. In addition, the coming Fourth Congress of the PAFL would be called on to attempt to have the Gómez government denounced by all the nations in the Western Hemisphere.[66]

In December 1923, following the Portland convention, the Executive Committee of the PAFL met to discuss the measures that had been taken to carry out the resolution on Venezuela of the Third Congress. The minutes of the committee show that on February 4, 1922, a communication had been sent to two unnamed labor organizations in Venezuela, but only one reply was received. It was dated March 30, 1922,

65. *Ibid. Proceedings*, 3rd PAFL Cong., p. 125.
66. Draft of the AFL resolution on Venezuela; GM.

and read in brief as follows: The rules of the organization did not allow members to discuss in their meetings questions relating to religion or politics. The officers of the organization would like to inform the PAFL of the status of the working class in Venezuela, but they dared not do so for fear that they would jeopardize their personal security as well as that of their organization. They suggested that the PAFL send a committee to Caracas and Maracaibo to investigate for itself. They sent a list of labor organizations in Venezuela, but asked that the source of this information not be revealed.[67] The PAFL report does not give the names of the persons who wrote this letter nor of the organization that they represented. On May 4, 1922, the PAFL sent letters of inquiry as to the status of the working people in Venezuela to the thirty organizations in the list sent by this unnamed organization. No answers to any of these letters were received, nor were any of them returned. On March 31, 1923, another series of letters was sent to the same organizations, but the result was the same as before. The Executive Committee then concluded that it would be impossible for them to get the information that they wished from Venezuela.[68]

The resolution of the AFL Portland convention brought a protest from Venezuela. On November 16, 1923, Jesús María Hernández, the president of the Confederación de Obreros y Artesanos del Distrito Federal in Caracas sent a cable to Gompers protesting the Muñoz Marín resolution and announcing that his organization was publishing a manifesto proclaiming the true state of affairs in Venezuela.[69]

The manifesto published by Hernández is in the form of a pamphlet. On the first page is a photograph of Gómez in the act of receiving a medal from a representative of the Confederación de Artesanos, Obreros, e Industriales de Vene-

67. Minutes of the Pan-American Federation of Labor Executive Committee Meeting, Dec. 5, 1923, annex 2; GM.
68. *Ibid.*, annex 2.
69. *Ibid.*, annex 3. Gompers to Jesús María Hernández, Dec. 6, 1923; GCB.

zuela in August 1922. Following is a five-page defense of
Gómez by Hernández himself. In his argument Hernández
denied that labor in Venezuela was in any way being mo-
lested. On the contrary, he stated that under Gómez labor had
prospered, and in many cases the wages of workers had
tripled. Furthermore, there were more jobs than there were
people to fill them; and as for hours of work, practically
everyone was on an eight-hour day. After thus praising
Gómez, Hernández ended by declaring that the anti-Gómez
propaganda being spread throughout the United States had
its origin in the personal ambitions of the enemies of Gómez.[70]

On December 6, 1923, Gompers sent Hernández a four-
page letter in reply to the pamphlet. He denied that the AFL
had accused the Gómez government as Hernández had implied, for while the Muñoz Marín resolution had listed alleged
crimes of the Gómez government, the AFL in accepting the
resolution had not made these allegations its own. He told
Hernández of the long list of unanswered letters which the
PAFL had sent to Venezuelan labor organizations, and he
noted that the Confederación de Obreros y Artesanos of which
Hernández was president was not included in that list. He
asked Hernández for information about the Confederación:
when it was formed, who were its officers, and what relation
it had with the labor movement of Venezuela. In closing his
letter, Gompers told Hernández that if the allegations listed
in the Muñoz Marín resolution were unfounded, no one could
object to the action that had been taken by the PAFL to determine the truth about labor conditions in Venezuela.[71]

In early January 1924 Gompers received a letter which he
hoped would help him obtain authentic information on
Gómez and his treatment of the workers in Venezuela. The

70. [Jesús María Hernández], *Mensaje de la Confederación de Obreros y
Artesanos del Distrito Federal a la American Federation of Labor y a todas
las Federaciones Obreras de América* (Tipo. Moderna, Caracas, 1923), pages
not numbered; IP.
71. Gompers to Jesús María Hernández, Dec. 6, 1923; GCB.

letter was signed by M. R. Morgan, an employee of the West-inghouse Electric International Company. Morgan wrote that he had recently been on a business trip to Venezuela and that he had been unfavorably impressed by what he had seen there. He told Gompers that he would be glad to place at his disposal information relating to Gómez that he had collected while he was in Venezuela.[72] Gompers sent a copy of this letter to Iglesias, who was in New York at this time, and asked him to act as his personal representative in a conference with Morgan.[73] On the same day he wrote Morgan that as he would not be available for a meeting for some time, he had arranged with Iglesias to act for him.[74]

Sometime during the latter part of January 1924, Iglesias had a conference with Morgan, who told him of his own personal experiences in Venezuela—unfortunately not recorded in the report of this meeting—and promised to give him further information after he had obtained it from his friends. However, Morgan apparently had difficulty in persuading his friends to release their information,[75] and what information Iglesias actually did obtain from him is not known. Whatever it was, it was never made public. The PAFL Executive Committee report to the Fourth Congress refers to numerous documents and letters on Venezuela which suggested that the charge which had been made against Gómez had some basis in fact, but it contains no specific mention of any information which had been obtained from Morgan. The Fourth Congress, while not pressing the previous charges made against Gómez, urged its affiliates to call the attention of their governments to the conditions existing in Venezuela.[76] One receives the impression that the charges against Gómez were exaggerated.

72. M. R. Morgan to Gompers, Jan. 7, 1924; GCB and IP.
73. Gompers to Iglesias, Jan. 17, 1924; GCB.
74. Gompers to M. R. Morgan, Jan. 17, 1924; GCB and IP.
75. M. R. Morgan to Iglesias, Jan. 22, 1924; IP.
76. *Proceedings*, 4th PAFL Cong., p. 121.

The letter dated March 30, 1922, which Gompers received from the unnamed labor organization in Venezuela caused something of a stir in the State Department. In publicizing this letter in New York's *La Prensa*, Gompers said that if anyone doubted its authenticity, he would be willing to submit it to Secretary of State Hughes for examination.[77] As the Gómez government had already protested to the United States against the action that Gompers had taken,[78] the State Department was becoming concerned over the whole matter. Undersecretary of State William Phillips suspected that someone connected with the United States diplomatic or consular service in Venezuela had played a part in transmitting the letter to Gompers. He therefore asked the American chargé d'affaires ad interim in Caracas to look into this possibility.[79] Apparently nothing came of this investigation, for it was not mentioned at the Fourth Congress some months later.

With the exception of Mexico and the countries just dealt with, the PAFL had few occasions to aid the labor movements of Latin America, although most of the Central American nations were at one time or another active to some degree in the organization.

Guatemala, with sixteen hundred organized workers in 1921,[80] was represented at the Laredo Conference and the Third and Fourth congresses. It had two labor federations recognized as bona fide by the PAFL: the Federación Obrera de Guatemala and the Federación Obrera Occidental. Guatemala played a major part in the formation of the Central American Federation of Labor, which was hoped to be a beginning move toward the political unification of the republics of Central America. The first step toward this organization was taken at the Second Congress of the PAFL in

77. William D. Phillips to Frederick C. Chabot, April 2, 1924; SD-NA.
78. Memorandum, Legación de los Estados Unidos de Venezuela, Jan. 24, 1924, protesting Gompers' and AFL propaganda against Venezuela; SD-NA.
79. William Phillips to Frederick C. Chabot, April 2, 1924; SD-NA.
80. *Proceedings*, 3rd PAFL Cong., p. 13.

1919 when the delegates from El Salvador obtained the adoption of a resolution for a Central American Federation of Labor. This resolution embraced in considerable detail the form that the organization was to assume.[81] It was not fully organized until September 1921, when it held its first congress in Guatemala City.[82]

Honduras was represented at the Second Congress of the PAFL by the Unión de Obreros, which claimed two thousand members in 1919.[83] It played a minor role in the PAFL and was not represented at subsequent congresses.

El Salvador was represented at Laredo and at the Second and Third congresses. Like Guatemala, it had two labor movements recognized as bona fide by the PAFL: the Unión Obrera Salvadoreña and the Federación Regional de Trabajadores de El Salvador, the combined membership of which was two thousand in 1919.[84] El Salvador played a modest part in the PAFL; its contribution to the Central American Federation of Labor gave it a position of prominence in its area.

In South America the PAFL was weaker by far than in Central America. The fact is that it hardly more than touched South America. Colombia was formally represented at the Laredo Conference, but did not have any delegates to succeeding congresses of the Gompers period. Peru, as we have already noted, played a major part in the Second Congress, but was not represented at succeeding congresses. Venezuela had a labor movement in exile beginning in 1925 which was called the Unión Obrera Venezolana, which was located in New York, and which sent delegates to the Fifth Congress in 1927.[85]

81. *Proceedings*, 2nd PAFL Cong., pp. 50-51.
82. *Proceedings*, 4th PAFL Cong., p. 49.
83. *Proceedings*, 2nd PAFL Cong., pp. 35, 59.
84. *Proceedings*, 2nd PAFL Cong., p. 59.
85. William Green to Rafael Iriarte, July 2, 1925; Green Copybooks, hereinafter abbreviated GrCB; AFL-CIO files. *Proceedings*, 5th PAFL Cong., *passim.*

# *Five.* Relations with Mexico

The Pan-American Federation of Labor was throughout its rather short history concerned first of all with the problems of Mexico. Through its representative labor organization, the Confederación Regional Obrera Mexicana, Mexico received more aid and attention from the PAFL than all the other Latin-American nations combined. The AFL and the CROM were usually in full agreement on all questions of major importance, although from time to time they found themselves temporarily at odds.

One of the problems confronting the PAFL was that of Latin-American immigration into the United States. The CROM was quite anxious to maintain freedom of movement between the United States and Mexico, at least of Mexicans into the United States. But Gompers was of a different opinion. For years he had attempted to restrict if not end all immigration into the United States. His first concern was the protection of United States labor; since a surplus of workers tended to lower wages, he opposed any measure or device that would increase the labor supply beyond that which was needed. He did not oppose immigration on principle. On the contrary, he believed that every person had the right to live, to work, or to travel anywhere in the world that he might choose, and he looked forward to the day when this would be possible. But he knew that from a practical point of view it would be best for the workers of all countries to fight for higher wages and better conditions on their own home ground rather than emigrate in an attempt to avoid the issue.

He looked upon uncontrolled immigration into the United States as a real menace to the American labor movement. At the same time, he was more than willing to help workers anywhere to better their conditions, and we have already seen that he did not rule out violence, even armed revolt, as a means of winning economic justice for the common people if all other methods failed. He insisted, however, that all workers everywhere should fight their own battles and not depend upon others for a solution of their problems.

Mexican immigration had been of importance long before the formation of the PAFL. As early as 1910, the Texas Federation of Labor, an AFL affiliate, had complained to Gompers of the importation into the United States of large numbers of poverty-stricken Mexican laborers by the railroads, building contractors, and labor agencies. Gompers had passed this complaint on to Daniel J. O'Keefe, the commissioner-general of immigration in Washington,[1] with a request for action. Evidently many of these immigrants were entering the United States without following lawful procedure, for O'Keefe replied that an effort was being made to bring illegal immigration from Mexico to an end.[2] The real problem of the AFL, however, was not that of illegal immigration, but of legal immigration directed by those irresponsible agencies listed by the Texas Federation of Labor, and the problem continued to be a source of potential dissension between the AFL and Mexican labor for many years to come.

We have already discussed the immigration issue as it was handled at the Second Congress of the PAFL when Gompers took a firm stand against immigration into the United States. The determination of Gompers to end or at least to reduce immigration put a stop for the time being to further discussion of the issue in the congresses of the PAFL. Nevertheless, it continued to be a subject of constant discussion by

1. Gompers to Daniel J. O'Keefe, April 28, 1910; GCB.
2. O'Keefe to Gompers, April 30, 1910; GCB.

the officers of the AFL and the PAFL. In 1920 it was brought up at a meeting of the AFL Executive Council in connection with a recent communication from Clemente I. Idar, the AFL representative in the Texas-Arizona area. Idar had reported to Vargas that a recently inaugurated open-shop drive in Texas and Arizona had been accompanied by new rulings of the Labor Department which allowed the importation of more Mexican workers of certain categories into the United States.[3] A year later Idar reported that he believed another demand would be made by employers in his area for more immigrant Mexican labor in the coming months. Gompers was especially disturbed at this possibility because of the large number of unemployed workers in the United States at the time.[4] Immigration was becoming one of the important political issues in the United States, with the AFL pressing for prohibition of immigration from all countries for a definite number of years. Gompers was more concerned with the influx of Europeans than that of Latin Americans, and the Executive Council under his leadership determined to investigate the possibility of inducing would-be immigrants to go to South Africa and British East Africa rather than come to the United States.[5] Nevertheless, the problem of Mexican immigration continued to exist, and it brought a visit from Morones in February 1922 to discuss the question with the AFL Executive Council and the officers of the PAFL.[6] However, not until after the death of Gompers in 1924 did the PAFL really come to grips with the problems of Mexican immigration.

Another problem of major importance to the PAFL was the constant danger of United States intervention in Mexico. After Mexico had adopted her new Constitution of 1917, this

3. AFL Executive Council Minutes, Aug. 7, 1920.
4. Gompers to Idar, July 28, 1921; GCB.
5. AFL Executive Council Minutes, March 1, 1921.
6. AFL Executive Council Minutes, Feb. 21, 1922.

danger increased because of the provisions it contained which could have injured foreign holders of Mexican land and oil and mineral rights. From 1917 on there seemed to be a deliberate propaganda campaign in the United States to press for action against Mexico. Mexican labor leaders believed that there was great danger of actual armed intervention by the United States, and this feeling was shared by the officers of the PAFL. Tension approached a climax in 1919 with the formation of a Senate subcommittee on foreign affairs to deal with the Mexican situation. This group was headed by Senator Albert B. Fall of New Mexico, an unsavory individual who conducted the hearings of the subcommittee in such a manner as to lead the American people to believe that armed intervention in Mexico was desirable. Both the AFL and the PAFL condemned the reports issued by the subcommittee as untrue.[7] Morones, supported by John Murray, asked the PAFL for aid in the crisis,[8] and the matter was brought to the attention of the Executive Council of the AFL by Gompers. Its decision was that the AFL would continue to aid Mexico and that the principles of "reason, fairness, and justice" would be applied in relations between the United States and Mexico.[9]

The situation became more difficult in December 1919 when United States Consular Agent William O. Jenkins—an adventurer who later made a fortune in Mexico through dubious means—was arrested in Puebla. Jenkins had allegedly been kidnapped by Mexican bandits, and the State Department had been unable to obtain his release through the Carranza government. Later, so he claimed, Jenkins had to ransom himself. As there was good reason to believe that

7. *Proceedings,* 2nd PAFL Cong., p. 62. *Proceedings,* 3rd PAFL Cong., pp. 55-59.
8. AFL Executive Council Minutes, Aug. 28, 1919.
9. *Ibid.* Gompers to Morones, Sept. 6, 1919; GCB. Gompers to Severino Bazán and Marcos A. Ochoa, Sept. 9, 1919; GCB. AFL Executive Council Minutes, Oct. 10, 1919. Gompers to Vargas, Oct. 20, 1919; GCB.

Jenkins was guilty of collusion with his "abductors," the Carranza government had him placed under arrest.[10] Gompers, with Vargas concurring, asked Carranza to release Jenkins immediately and unconditionally.[11] Jenkins was released the day following Gompers' appeal and for some time the atmosphere was slightly cleared.

The next crisis between Mexico and the United States came in the summer of 1921. At this time there was a strike of Mexican oil workers in progress in the Tampico area,[12] a region in which United States interests were especially powerful. As the State Department had received reports of possible disturbances in that vicinity, it had asked for military aid to protect American life and property. Two naval vessels were consequently dispatched to Tampico.[13] It so happened that two AFL leaders, E. C. Davidson and John Kelly, were attending a CROM convention being held in Orizaba at that time, and—no doubt influenced by the CROM leadership—they immediately appealed to Gompers to protest the presence of the warships to Secretary of State Hughes. Gompers therefore called a meeting of the PAFL Executive Committee to deal with the issue. The decision of the committee was to ask Hughes to state publicly that the vessels were not in Tampico for the purpose of interfering with the striking Mexican workers.[14] Hughes made the requested statement in a letter to Gompers[15] and in a note to Mexican Ambassador Manuel C. Téllez.[16] The response of Hughes to Gompers was greeted in the CROM convention with cries of "Viva Gompers!"[17] After reporting to Tampico, the warships were withdrawn from the area.[18]

10. Howard F. Cline, *The United States and Mexico* (Cambridge, Mass., 1953), pp. 190-191.
11. Gompers to Carranza, Dec. 4, 1919; GCB.
12. Gompers to Hughes, July 7, 1921; SD-NA.
13. Richard C. Tanis to Manuel C. Téllez, July 13, 1921; SD-NA.
14. Gompers to Hughes, July 7, 1921; GCB.
15. Hughes to Gompers, July 8, 1921; SD-NA.
16. Richard C. Tanis to Manuel C. Téllez, July 13, 1921; SD-NA.
17. PAFL Executive Committee Minutes, July 16, 1921; GM.
18. Richard C. Tanis to Manuel C. Téllez, July 13, 1921; SD-NA.

Early in 1920, after it had become clear that President Venustiano Carranza intended to remain in office indefinitely, Alvaro Obregón took up arms against his former leader. By May 1920 Obregón had captured Mexico City and Carranza had fled eastward, only to lose his life before he could reach Veracruz. The death of Carranza seriously weakened the position of the friends of the Mexican Revolution in the United States who were fighting against American intervention. Inasmuch as Carranza had met his death under conditions which suggested that he had been murdered by his political enemies, the United States felt justified in withholding recognition of both Adolfo de la Huerta, the provisional president, and Alvaro Obregón, the regularly elected president who took office in December 1920. Those persons in the United States who wanted to see a change in the Mexican Constitution of 1917 which would guarantee the property rights of foreigners in Mexico believed that they could use recognition as a means of forcing the Obregón government to accede to their demands. As they were well represented in the conservative and corrupt Harding government, they were in a position to demand as the price of recognition a treaty which would guarantee in advance the oil and mineral rights of foreigners as they had existed prior to the adoption of Article 27 of the Mexican Constitution, which states that the products of the subsoil belong to the nation. Gompers, of course, had asked Hughes to support the recognition of Obregón during the first year that Hughes had been in office, and he had mentioned in a letter to Morones that he had assured Hughes that the Obregón government could not legally be a party to such a treaty as the State Department had proposed.[19] At the annual convention of the AFL in June 1922, James Lord, now the treasurer of the PAFL and a delegate to the AFL convention, introduced a resolution asking that the United States recognize the Obregón government. This resolution was duly

19. Gompers to Morones, Dec. 22, 1921; GCB,

adopted and copies were sent to Secretary Hughes and other interested government officials.[20]

Negotiations between the United States and Mexico regarding recognition continued on into 1923 when a commission was formed in the United States to confer with a similar Mexican commission on the questions of recognition and the rights of foreigners in Mexico. Gompers and Vargas were anxious to have a labor representative on the American commission, but an appeal to Hughes brought no results. Hughes claimed that there were so many applications for representation on the commission that he had found it necessary to disregard all petitions from all sources. He further claimed that if labor were given representation, a precedent would be established which would work to the detriment of the commission.[21] Vargas then suggested to Gompers that the problem be approached through General Plutarco Elías Calles, the Ministro de Gobernación in Obregón's cabinet. A telegram was therefore sent to Calles suggesting that James Lord be sent to Mexico City, where the commissions were to convene, for the purpose of aiding both of the commissions as well as he might.[22] A letter and telegram were at the same time sent to Lord, who was in California, telling him of the measures that had been taken. His status at the conferences was to be that of an observer representing the PAFL, although it was implied that he would be paid by the Obregón government.[23] Apparently Calles replied in the affirmative to the telegram sent to him, for by May 15 Lord was in Mexico City and had made his first report to Gompers. At this time the American and Mexican commissioners were still only expressing feelings of mutual good will. Lord found that he would be unable to attend the meetings of the commission-

20. Gompers to Hughes, July 1, 1922; SD-NA and GCB. Gompers to Coolidge, July 1, 1922; GCB. Draft of AFL Resolution Number 31, introduced by James Lord; GCB. AFL Executive Council Minutes, Sept. 9-16, 1922. *Proceedings,* 4th PAFL Cong., p. 25.
21. Minutes of a Conference of Gompers and Vargas, May 4, 1923; GM.
22. *Ibid.*
23. PAFL Executive Committee to James Lord, May 4, 1923; GCB.

ers—the so-called Bucareli conferences—for they were closed to observers. However, he arranged to talk to both the American and the Mexican representatives and furnished them with a memorandum containing the views of both the AFL and the PAFL on recognition.[24] In a press interview he made these views known to the general public. He was confident that the conferences would result in the recognition of the Obregón government.[25]

The confidence of Lord was vindicated by the announcement on August 31, 1923, that diplomatic relations between the United States and Mexico had been restored.[26] But the Bucareli conferences cost the PAFL one of its officers, for James Lord ruined his health during the early weeks of the negotiations.[27] A month after he had arrived in Mexico City he had suffered a nervous breakdown which had left him completely helpless.[28] He was cared for by the CROM[29] until Vargas arrived from the United States to conduct him back to California.[30] A year later he had regained his health,[31] but as he did not feel able to continue his work as treasurer of the PAFL, he resigned.[32]

Only a few weeks after the accession of Obregón to the presidency, the PAFL met in Mexico City for its Third Congress. This action emphasized PAFL support of the new government. The business sessions of the PAFL were held in the National Preparatory School during the period January 10-18, 1921.[33] Although a large amount of routine business was transacted, there was none of the dissension that had marked

24. *Proceedings*, 4th PAFL Cong., p. 27.
25. James Lord to Gompers, May 15, 1923; GCB.
26. Gompers to Hughes, Sept. 1, 1923; GCB. Gompers to Obregón, Sept. 1, 1923; GCB and GM. Gompers to Eduardo Moneda. Sept. 1, 1923; GCB and GM.
27. Gompers to U. S. Consul in Mexico City, June 19, 1923; SD-NA.
28. Wright to A. W. Kliefoth, June 19, 1923; SD-NA.
29. J. Butler Wright to Gompers, June 26, 1923; SD-NA.
30. Gompers to Joseph Lord, July 7, 1923; GCB.
31. Gompers to Vargas, Aug. 21, 1924; GCB.
32. James Lord to Gompers, Oct. 28, 1924; GCB. Gompers to Vargas, Oct. 31, 1924; GCB. James Lord to Gompers, Oct. 28, 1924; GCB. Gompers to James Lord, Oct. 31, 1924; GCB.
33. *Proceedings*, 3rd PAFL Cong., *passim*.

the two previous conventions. The success of Obregón had apparently left the delegates in a congenial and festive frame of mind. One of the highlights of the congress was a dinner for the delegates given by General Calles at the San Angel Inn on the outskirts of Mexico City,[34] and at the business session of the congress several speeches were made by prominent persons invited for this purpose. The most colorful of these was given by Mrs. Mary Jones, the noted American radical of the early part of this century known as "Mother" Jones who had played such an inspiring role in organizing the American coal miners. She had come to Mexico at the invitation of Obregón, and Gompers introduced her to the congress as a "magnificent" woman affiliated with the United Mine Workers of America.[35] In a short speech well suited to her audience, she emphasized the unity of working people everywhere regardless of their political philosophy.[36]

One of the resolutions adopted by the Third Congress tended to negate the stand taken by Gompers at the Laredo Conference in regard to the members of the IWW who were at that time in prison in the United States, and it prepared the way for later action by the PAFL on matters relating to political prisoners. The case dealt with by the Third Congress was that of Augustin L. Sánchez, a Mexican member of the AFL Shipbuilders Lodge of Buffalo, New York.[37] Sánchez was at the time of the Third Congress awaiting execution for murder[38] along with an alleged accomplice, Enrique García,[39] at the New York penitentiary in Ossining. Five days before the execution date, the Third Congress appealed to New York's Governor Nathan Miller asking for pardons for Sánchez and García, but all appeals were in vain and both of the men were

34. *Ibid.*
35. *Ibid.*
36. *Ibid.*
37. Gompers to Mrs. Francis L. Sánchez, May 29, 1920; GCB.
38. *Proceedings*, 3rd PAFL Cong., p. 107.
39. Owen L. Potter to Governor Alfred E. Smith, Aug. 19, 1920; GCB.

executed,[40] despite the fact that Sánchez was believed by the PAFL to be innocent and there was every reason to believe that García was mentally incompetent.[41]

The Sánchez-García case was related to a miscarriage of justice rather than to politics, but while it was being considered, the question of the release of Juan Cabral, a prisoner at Leavenworth Penitentiary who had been convicted of violating the espionage laws of the United States, was brought to the attention of Gompers, first by Morones and then by Antonio I. Villarreal. The basis of their appeal for the release of Cabral was that the other persons involved in the case who had been convicted along with Cabral had already been released. Gompers asked Secretary of State Bainbridge Colby to consider the justice of releasing Cabral.[42]

The Cabral case was followed two years later by the involvement of the PAFL in a movement to obtain freedom for Ricardo Flores Magón and other persons connected with the Los Angeles Junta of the Mexican Liberal party who were still in prison for violation of the neutrality laws of the United States during the Mexican Revolution.[43] This interest in political prisoners led to a resolution adopted by the Fourth Congress in 1924 which asked the governor of Texas to pardon Abraham Cisneros, Jesús M. Rangel, Jesús González, Leonardo M. Vásquez, Pedro Perales, and Charles Cline, all of whom had been condemned to life imprisonment as the result of the killing of a member of a sheriff's posse on the Mexican border during the Revolution.[44] As these men were all revolutionary heroes, it is understandable that there was a great desire to have them released.

40. *Proceedings,* 3rd PAFL Cong., p. 107.
41. Gompers to Governor Alfred E. Smith, Dec. 20, 1920; GCB.
42. Gompers to Bainbridge Colby, July 10, 1920; GCB. Gompers to Antonio I. Villarreal, July 10, 1920; GCB.
43. Vargas to Pedro Ramírez, Nov. 24, 1922; IP. Pedro Ramírez to Vargas, Nov. 15, 1922; IP.
44. *Proceedings,* 4th PAFL Cong., p. 112.

In 1922 the Mexican labor movement paid off a portion of its debt to the AFL for aid down through the years by supporting the strike of AFL railway shopmen in the United States. As in every strike, the major problem of the shopmen was to prevent the use of strikebreakers, to win the sympathy and support of other unions and the general public, and to maintain themselves and their families for the duration of the strike. Employers in the border states had in the past used Mexican labor whenever possible in situations of this kind, but in 1922 the existence of the PAFL made it impossible for the railroads in that area to hire Mexican "scabs" to replace the American strikers. Under the leadership of the CROM, August 1 was set aside for parades, demonstrations, and meetings throughout Mexico in support of the shopmen. The Unión de Mecánicos Mexicanos in Aguascalientes and the Confederación de Sociedades Ferrocarrileras de la República de México in Mexico City issued a manifesto in support of the shopmen which called upon the Mexicans to aid the American strikers by refusing to accept jobs left vacant by the strike. The Mexican Consul-General in San Antonio, Texas, warned all Mexicans that if they acted as strikebreakers they did so at their own risk. The Mexican trade unionists in Ciudad Juárez sponsored an amateur bullfight for the benefit of the shopmen in El Paso.[45] In addition, the Mexican railway unions sent a thousand pesos to the strikers, and paymasters on several Mexican lines were ordered by their unions to set aside two and a half pesos per capita for some thirty-five thousand employees to form a benefit fund for the strikers.[46]

The ties between Mexican labor and the AFL were greatly strengthened by Mexican support of the shopmen and by the phenomenal growth of the CROM during the Obregón administration. Gompers was in full agreement with the

45. Vargas to Gompers, Aug. 1, 1922; GCB.
46. Gompers to B. M. Jewell, Sept. 16, 1922; GCB.

Obregón labor policy, and as election time drew near in Mexico, he began a campaign to assure the continuation of this policy for at least another four years. In September 1923, shortly after Obregón had been recognized by the United States, he had suggested to CROM Secretary-General Eduardo Moneda that the time had come for a meeting of the Executive Committee of the PAFL and representatives of the CROM to exchange "views and impressions." He suggested that the meeting be held in El Paso, Texas, on October 24 or 25, which would be immediately following the AFL annual convention.[47] The CROM accepted the invitation[48] and on October 25 the first of a series of conferences was held in the Hotel Paso del Norte, in El Paso. Present as representatives of the PAFL were Gompers, Wright, and Vargas. The CROM was represented by Samuel O. Yúdico, Reynaldo Cervantes Torres, Fernando Rodarte, and Roberto Haberman. Iglesias was also present, as was W. C. Roberts, secretary to Gompers.[49] Iglesias was formally representing the Federación Libre of Puerto Rico, but his presence in El Paso was in reality due to his unofficial position of adviser to Gompers on Latin-American affairs. After the usual preliminaries, the meeting settled down to business and the reason for the meeting soon became apparent. In a carefully-worded statement to the conference, Gompers said that if he were a Mexican he would do everything in his power to assure the election of Calles, the choice of Obregón, and he urged the CROM to give full support to Calles, but at the same time to preserve its political identity. He then told the conference that the AFL convention just concluded in Portland had decided to hold its 1924 convention in El Paso and that it had occurred to a number of persons that it would be appropriate if the CROM were

47. Gompers to Eduardo Moneda, Sept. 20, 1923; GCB.
48. Gompers to Vargas, Oct. 5, 1923; GCB. Gompers to Ricardo Treviño, Oct. 5, 1923; GCB.
49. Minutas de las conferencias celebradas en el Hotel Paso del Norte, El Paso, Texas, los días 25, 26, y 27 de octubre de 1923; IP.

to hold its convention in adjoining Ciudad Juárez at the same time. He further suggested that the next congress of the PAFL be held in Ciudad Juárez immediately following the AFL and CROM conventions. Roberto Haberman then proposed that inasmuch as the election of Calles was a foregone conclusion, and as his inauguration would take place in Mexico City on December 1, 1924, it would be well if the PAFL were to meet in Mexico City at that time rather than in Ciudad Juárez. After a long discussion, Haberman's proposal was adopted. A formal resolution was thereafter drafted explaining to the PAFL affiliates why the Fourth Congress was to meet in Mexico City rather than Guatemala, the site which had been chosen by the Third Congress. The chief reason given for this change was that political conditions in Guatemala at that time made it impracticable to meet there. It was agreed, however, that if there should be a change in Guatemala favorable to a meeting of the congress there, the first two days of the meeting would be spent in Mexico City and the remainder in Guatemala. This would make it possible for the delegates to attend the inauguration of Calles,[50] an event presumably of great significance to Latin-American labor. Another day was spent by the El Paso conference in discussing the IFTU, but as the discussion was of a general nature and as it did not affect the PAFL—at least as far as the records show—it will not be treated here.

Gompers gave all possible publicity to his support of Calles. In a letter to Morones as secretary-general of the Partido Laborista Mexicano, he repeated his statement to the El Paso conference and added that he hoped to be present when Calles was inducted into office.[51] In a press release to the New York *Times*, he told of the El Paso conference and how the CROM with its 800,000 members was backing Calles, whom he called the exponent of "the principles of freedom,

50. *Ibid.*
51. Gompers to Morones, Oct. 27, 1923; GCB.

democracy, and human progress."[52] He added that while the AFL had no right to interfere in the affairs of a neighboring country, it could not refrain from expressing its hope that a friend of labor and democracy would be elected in Mexico.[53] Calles was understandably pleased with this declaration, and in a telegram expressing his appreciation for the stand that Gompers had taken, he praised him as "the old paladin of human liberties and the forever firm defender of the interests of the workers."[54]

Less than a month after Gompers had announced that the PAFL would support Calles, a revolt broke out in Mexico. The political leader of the revolt was Adolfo de la Huerta, who had been provisional president of Mexico following the ousting of Carranza, and who no doubt had hoped to become the legal successor to Obregón were an honest election held. His chief military supporters were General Guadalupe Sánchez of Veracruz and General Enrique Estrada of Jalisco. The revolt began on December 6, 1925,[55] and it was not broken until some months later. Among a number of prominent persons in the revolutionary movement who were backing de la Huerta were Antonio I. Villarreal[56] and Salvador Alvarado,[57] two early supporters of the PAFL movement whom we have already mentioned.

Two days after the revolt began, CROM Secretary Ricardo Treviño appealed to Gompers for aid. In his appeal Treviño declared that the object of de la Huerta was to overthrow Obregón and to inaugurate a period of reaction. He further declared that the CROM was throwing all of its strength behind Obregón and that steps had been taken to form contingents of trade unionists for service in the field. He ap-

52. AFL press release to New York *Times*, Nov. 8, 1923; GM.
53. *Ibid.*
54. Plutarco Elías Calles to Gompers, Nov. 11, 1923; GM and IP.
55. *Proceedings*, 4th PAFL Cong., p. 34.
56. Miguel Angel Peral, *Diccionario biográfico mexicano* (México, 1944), p. 863.
57. *Ibid.*, p. 44.

pealed to Gompers as chairman of the PAFL to use his influence to prevent aid from reaching de la Huerta from his followers in the United States.[58] A similar appeal was made by Morones.[59]

The reply of the PAFL leaders to these appeals was prompt and unequivocal. They pledged full support to Obregón and praised him as a patriot and a sincere friend of the Mexican wage earners. They declared that the Obregón government was the best that Mexico had ever had. They condemned any and all attempts to overthrow democratic governments anywhere, and they branded the de la Huerta revolt as an effort of a group of extreme reactionaries supported by a powerful body of revolutionists of the "communist or bolshevik" type to attempt to gain by rebellion what it could never legally gain at the polls.[60]

Immediately following the outbreak of the revolt Morones sent Roberto Haberman to the United States as his personal agent and general representative of the Mexican government. It appears that the chief duty of Haberman was to take all possible steps to prevent arms and ammunition from reaching de la Huerta from the United States or Europe.[61] After conferring with Haberman, Gompers wrote Secretary of State Hughes that he had been reliably informed that de la Huerta had been receiving arms from some illegal source in the United States. He added, however, that he was not positive that this report was true. He suggested to Hughes that such action was a violation of the wishes of the United States government, and he intimated—with an amazing degree of presumptuousness—that Hughes himself should be supporting Obregón.[62]

58. AFL press release, Dec. 11, 1923; GM.
59. *Proceedings*, 4th PAFL Cong., p. 34.
60. Gompers to Ricardo Treviño and Reynaldo Cervantes Torres, Dec. 11, 1923; GCB.
61. *Proceedings*, 4th PAFL Cong., p. 36.
62. Gompers to Hughes, Dec. 18, 1923; SD-NA and GCB. Gompers to

The next move made by Gompers was to enlist the aid of United States labor in support of Obregón. In a lengthy statement directed especially to workers in the transportation and freight-handling industries, he appealed for help in detecting any shipments of arms and ammunition to de la Huerta. In his appeal he painted de la Huerta in the darkest possible colors. "The avowed purpose of the rebel de la Huerta, tool of reaction," he said, "is to crush the labor movement, to enforce compulsory labor by denying the right of workmen to leave their work, to give back the public land to great concessionaries, to set Mexico back a decade or more into darkness."[63] This may have been the secret intention of de la Huerta, but it was certainly not his "avowed" purpose, as Gompers well knew. The wording of this passage leads one to believe that it was not the work of Gompers, but probably that of Roberto Haberman.

As arms smuggling seemed most likely to occur in those seaports closest to Mexico, Gompers dispatched Clemente I. Idar to the Galveston–Beaumont–Port Arthur area to investigate the possibility of arms being passed through those ports. He told Idar that all evidence which indicated that arms were being smuggled through this area should first be given to the local representatives of the federal government and then telegraphed to AFL headquarters so that Gompers could convey it directly to the proper officials in Washington.[64]

A second possible source of arms for the rebels was Europe, and Gompers therefore next directed his attention to European labor through the International Federation of Trade Unions. In a cablegram to IFTU headquarters in Amsterdam, Gompers and the other members of the PAFL Executive Committee explained the nature of the de la Huerta revolt and stated that they did not believe that any European govern-

Ricardo Treviño, Dec. 18, 1923; GCB.
63. *Proceedings*, 4th PAFL Cong., p. 37.
64. Gompers to Idar, Dec. 21, 1923; GCB.

ment would allow its nationals to send arms to the rebels.[65] This communication did not call on the IFTU for aid, at least not in words. Nevertheless, the IFTU immediately replied that it had requested all of its affiliates to look into the matter.[66] As it was clear that the IFTU was more than willing to co-operate with the PAFL—despite the coolness which had existed between its leaders and Gompers for a number of years—Vargas informed its officers that while de la Huerta would probably attempt to obtain war supplies throughout Europe, the greatest danger was that he would find them in England and in Germany. Vargas suggested that the IFTU affiliates, especially the International Federation of Transport Workers, be on the alert, and he requested that the IFTU publicize throughout Europe the Treviño–Cervantes Torres letter to Gompers which showed the support that the Obregón government was receiving from the CROM.[67]

Toward the end of January 1924 the IFTU reported that it had received only one reply to its request for information on the arms question, but that it would continue its efforts to do all in its power to co-operate with the PAFL.[68] A week later it had received replies from the trade-union centers of England, Spain, and Sweden, and also from the International Trade Secretariats of the miners, woodworkers, and transport workers. None of these organizations knew of any arms shipments to Mexico, but they promised to continue to be on the alert for evidence. At this time the IFTU again pledged support to the PAFL and promised to send further information when it arrived.[69]

In the meantime the conflict in Mexico continued. On the day following the outbreak of the revolt, the CROM had called on its affiliates to prepare for armed service if such should become necessary. By early January 1924, according to a source favorable to the Obregón government, a special

65. *Proceedings*, 4th PAFL Cong., p. 40.
66. *Ibid.*        67. *Ibid.*        68. *Ibid.*        69. *Ibid.*

guard of a hundred members of the CROM was on duty at Chapultepec Palace, the official residence of President Obregón. Aguascalientes was being policed by two thousand peasants who were members of organizations affiliated to the CROM, and other towns in Zacatecas were being similarly protected.[70] The defeat of the rebels was only a matter of time.

By the middle of January the rebels were trying to win the sympathy of the PAFL. De la Huerta denied that he had played any part in the recent and highly publicized execution of Governor Felipe Carrillo Puerto of Yucatán, an Obregón supporter, and he invited Gompers and his followers to come to Veracruz at the expense of the rebel movement to determine for themselves the truth of the situation.[71] Similar invitations were extended by other persons associated with the de la Huerta movement.[72]

Apparently de la Huerta believed that there was at least the possibility of neutralizing Gompers and the PAFL, and such an optimistic view would not have been without foundation. Villarreal had been in close touch with PAFL leadership for many years and he had been known to Gompers since as far back as 1908.[73] Salvador Alvarado had been a pioneer in the PAFL movement[74] and had given invaluable moral and financial aid while it was being organized. De la Huerta himself had been an interested and presumably sympathetic observer of the movement since 1918,[75] although he had played no direct part in its organization or operation. He seems to have been taken aback by Gompers' vehement condemnation of the revolt, and he emphatically denied that he was an enemy of labor as Gompers had charged.[76] It was

70. AFL press release, Jan. 3, 1924; GM.
71. Adolfo de la Huerta to Gompers, Jan. 12, 1924; IP.
72. AFL press release, Jan. 3, 1924; IP.
73. Cf. page 4 above.
74. Cf. p. 21 above.
75. *Pan-American Labor Press*, Aug. 4, 1918.
76. Adolfo de la Huerta to Gompers, Jan. 12, 1924; IP.

Villarreal, however, who made the strongest plea for Gompers' support:

> In view of the fact that the leaders of the American Federation of Labor through their lack of knowledge as to the internal affairs of Mexico have made the serious mistake of supporting the candidacy of Calles, I am addressing you in the name of our old comradeship to ask that you rectify your position. Calles is a simulator, not a friend of labor or of the farmer. As you well know, he ordered the execution in Sonora of Lázaro Gutiérrez de Lara, the precursor of socialism in Mexico. The overwhelming majority of the agrarians have joined our movement, as well as almost all the trade unions with the exception of those under the direction of leaders who are on the government pay-roll. Our movement against the imposition [*sic*] will safeguard the social gains recognized in our Constitution. Hoping that you will very soon be convinced of your error, I salute you fraternally. General Antonio I. Villarreal.[77]

Gompers was not influenced by this communication or by others of a similar nature that he received from the rebels.[78] He accused them of showing duplicity by pretending to the labor movement that they were "reds" while they were at the same time making promises to business that they would render inoperative Articles 27 and 123 of the Mexican Constitution as far as labor and agrarian reforms were concerned. Jorge Prieto Laurens, one of the chief supporters of de la Huerta, had told Gompers that the object of the rebellion was to bring about "the socialization of the land and of the instruments of production" and that the movement had the support of the Mexican "reds";[79] but at the same time Enrique Seldner, the representative of de la Huerta who was operating in both New York and Washington, published a statement in the American press charging that the Obregón-

---

77. Antonio I. Villarreal to Gompers, Jan. 12, 1924; IP.
78. AFL press release, Jan. 31, 1924; GM and IP. Gompers to Obregón, Jan. 29, 1924; SD-NA and IP.
79. *Ibid.*

Calles combination was so tainted with red tendencies that Mexico would be converted into a soviet state dominated by Moscow if the revolt were to fail.[80]

At one point Gompers attempted to interest the State Department in a protest against the action of the followers of de la Huerta in Yucatán. In late February 1924 he asked Secretary of State Hughes to have the United States consul in Mérida look into the case of the family and political associates of the late Governor Felipe Carrillo Puerto, who were in danger of losing their lives at the hands of the de la Huertistas. This group included three members of the Yucatán legislature who had supported Obregón: Elvira Carrillo, the sister of the governor; Betty Peniche de Ponce; and Raquely Dzib y Cirerol.[81] Under-Secretary of State William Phillips replied for Hughes that inasmuch as the persons named by Gompers were "naturals of Yucatán," the United States could not intervene.[82]

By this time there was no longer any great danger that the rebels would be successful in overthrowing the Obregón government. Except for scattered guerilla action the revolt had been brought under control.[83] The IFTU had reported that there had been no arms shipments to the rebels from Europe,[84] and the vigilance of the PAFL had no doubt made it impossible for them to receive aid from their allies in the United States. Loss of life had not been great on either side, although both the rebels and the supporters of Obregón had suffered the loss of a number of relatively prominent persons. Among these was General Salvador Alvarado of Yucatán.[85]

The defeat of de la Huerta assured the election of Calles in

80. *Ibid.*
81. Gompers to Hughes, Feb. 25, 1924; SD-NA.
82. William Phillips to Gompers, March 4, 1924; IP.
83. Vargas to International Federation of Trade Unions, Feb. 19, 1924; quoted in *Proceedings,* 4th PAFL Cong., p. 42.
84. International Federation of Trade Unions to Vargas, Feb. 16, 1924; quoted in *Proceedings,* 4th PAFL Cong., p. 41.
85. Miguel Angel Peral, *Diccionario biográfico mexicano,* p. 863.

July 1924. Soon after his election he visited the United States. At a luncheon given in his honor by the Executive Council of the AFL in Atlantic City, he was praised by Gompers as being "one hundred per cent" and the Executive Council adopted a resolution to wire the CROM congratulating it and the Mexican people on his victory.[86] In October following, Roberto Haberman appeared before the AFL Executive Council to invite its members to attend the coming presidential inauguration in Mexico City at the expense of the Mexican government.[87]

In November 1924, while Gompers was preparing to leave for El Paso to arrange for the coming AFL convention there, he received word that Luis Morones had been wounded in a shooting affray which had occurred in the Chamber of Deputies in Mexico City. With Morones incapacitated, the CROM found it necessary to send Eduardo Moneda and Juan Rico to El Paso to discuss with Gompers plans for the coming AFL and CROM meetings.[88] The absence of Morones no doubt put an additional burden on Gompers and contributed to his rapidly failing health. During the El Paso meetings he was taken seriously ill and was forced to remain in his room the greater part of the time.[89] His illness came as no surprise as he had suffered a physical breakdown at the Democratic National Convention the preceding summer.[90] By mid-July he had recovered sufficiently to work an hour or so a day,[91] and in early November he had notified the CROM that he expected to be able to participate in the coming conventions and inauguration ceremonies.[92]

86. Minutes of a luncheon given by the Executive Council of the AFL for Calles, Atlantic City, Aug. 8, 1924; GM.
87. AFL Executive Council Minutes, Oct. 20, 1924.
88. Gompers to Reynaldo Cervantes Torres, Nov. 11, 1924; GCB. AFL press release, Nov. 15, 1924; GM.
89. Gompers to Mrs. Sara Conboy, Nov. 19, 1924; GM.
90. News item in *Justicia,* 11 de agosto de 1924, p. 1.
91. [Lee Guard?] to Vargas, July 16, 1924; GCB. [Lee Guard?] to Vargas, July 17, 1924; GCB.
92. Gompers to Ricardo Treviño, Nov. 5, 1924; GCB.

When the Fourth Congress of the PAFL convened at the National Museum in Mexico City on December 3, 1924, Gompers—despite his illness—was in the chair. Only five nations were officially represented: the United States, Mexico, Panama, Nicaragua, and the Dominican Republic. Two representatives of the Unificación Obrera Cooperativista of Guatemala were seated as fraternal delegates. The first sessions were devoted to short speeches by several persons, including two representatives of the British Trade Union Congress, A. B. Swales and C. T. Crump, and Spencer Miller, Jr., of the AFL Workers Education Bureau.[93] A thorough report of the de la Huerta revolt was made and many documents relating to the aid given by the IFTU were made part of the record.[94] The Nicaraguan question was also reported on in great detail.[95]

Among the thirty-odd resolutions adopted by the Fourth Congress were six that deserve special mention. Resolution 3, which was an amended version of a more detailed proposal made by the delegation from Panama, called on the United States and Great Britain to take measures to alleviate conditions in Panama due to the presence there of large numbers of workers from Jamaica and Barbados.[96] This was the first PAFL resolution involving a European power. Resolution 5 called on the labor organizations of Pan-America to support the Calles government.[97] Resolution 6 provided for a commission of three members—one each from the United States, Mexico, and the Caribbean—whose expenses would be borne by the AFL and the CROM, to carry out an intensive campaign of labor organization in Central and South America.[98] The old question of the exchange of union cards again came up for discussion and it was decided in Resolution 6 that the

93. *Proceedings,* 4th PAFL Cong., pp. 3-13.
94. *Ibid.,* pp. 24-46.
95. *Ibid.,* pp. 66-104.
96. *Ibid.,* p. 112.
97. *Ibid.,* p. 113.
98. *Ibid.,* p. 113.

AFL and CROM would urge their affiliates to examine the possibility of solving this knotty problem, which had been a subject of controversy since 1918.[99]

With one exception, the resolutions presented to the Fourth Congress were handled very quietly. The exception was Resolution 30, which had been introduced by Tómas S. González and Alfredo Cifuentes, the fraternal delegates from Guatemala. This resolution consisted of four parts: (1) that a mixed commission be sent to Central America to investigate the true status and condition of labor organizations there and to lend aid whenever possible to Central American movements of a social nature; (2) that no Central American government be recognized if it did not offer complete liberty to the labor movement; (3) that absolute observance of the law be demanded of Central American governments; (4) and that the PAFL demand of all Central American governments that the death penalty and infamous punishments like the lash be abolished. Since this resolution was one that would require considerable study before it could be put into effect, the resolutions committee recommended that the proposals be referred to the Executive Committee of the PAFL for consideration. Delegate González objected to thus disposing of the resolution and told the gathering that referring it to the Executive Council was tantamount to rejection. Delegate Fernando Rodarte of the CROM defended the action of the resolutions committee and in the course of his talk angered González by strongly implying that until the labor movements in the Central American countries had grown sufficiently strong to be able to put effective pressure on their respective governments, they should not call for help of this nature from the PAFL. González insisted that the resolution be adopted, but it was finally disposed of as the resolutions committee had recommended.[100]

99. *Ibid.*, p. 140.
100. *Ibid.*, pp. 126-139.

By December 8 Gompers was desperately ill and unable to attend the sessions. His place in the chair was taken by subordinates who terminated the congress with the unanimous re-election of Gompers, Morones, Wright, and Vargas.[101] On December 11 Gompers was removed by train from Mexico City to San Antonio, Texas, where he died on December 13, 1924.[102]

101. *Ibid.,* p. 146.
102. A full account of the illness and death of Samuel Gompers is given on page 1 of the New York *Times,* Dec. 9-13, 1924.

## *Six.* Decline and End

When Gompers died, it was rumored that Morones, by virtue of his position as vice-president of the PAFL, would succeed to the presidency;[1] but as no provision had been made in the constitution for succession in case of the death of an incumbent, the office was tendered by the leaders of the organization to William Green, the new president of the American Federation of Labor. Green formally accepted the position on February 25, 1925.[2]

Another change in the leadership of the PAFL occurred about the same time. Canuto A. Vargas, who had been the Spanish-language secretary of the organization since its inception, was appointed by President Calles in the spring of 1925 to the post of labor attaché on the staff of the Mexican embassy in Washington. Calles no doubt took this action in response to a resolution introduced by the AFL at the Fourth Congress of the PAFL which urged all Pan-American governments to accord representation to labor in their consular establishments.[3] Vargas had the distinction of being the first person in history to thus represent a labor movement.[4] Since he could not continue devoting his full time to the PAFL as its constitution required, it was necessary for him to resign.[5] The Executive Committee of the PAFL then submitted to Eduardo Moneda, at that time the secretary-general of the

1. New York *Times*, Dec. 15, 1924.
2. *Proceedings*, 5th PAFL Cong., p. 21.
3. *Proceedings*, 4th PAFL Cong., pp. 114-115.
4. *Proceedings*, 5th PAFL Cong., p. 22.
5. William Green to Eduardo Moneda, April 10, 1925; GrCB.

CROM, a request that the CROM nominate a successor to Vargas.[6] The CROM then nominated Santiago Iglesias,[7] who was also the choice of the PAFL Executive Committee.[8] Iglesias, however, was not without doubts as to the wisdom of accepting the post. He was already fully occupied with his work in Puerto Rico and he could not give full time to the PAFL. After considerable delay, he accepted the position with the understanding that part of his time would be spent in Puerto Rico in connection with his activities there.[9] He still had not reported for duty in Washington by the middle of July 1925, but he was there for a conference on Mexican immigration in the latter part of August.[10]

Throughout its history the PAFL was plagued with the problem of Mexican immigration into the United States. The problem had existed long before the PAFL had been formed, and it has persisted down to the present time. The problem of European immigration was solved by the quota system adopted in 1924, but this law did not apply to Latin Americans. Various restrictive devices were used by the United States authorities to control Mexican immigration as the situation demanded, but the AFL was by no means satisfied with the results. The problem had become intensified in early 1925 when Clemente N. Idar wrote William Green that Mexican immigration into the border states was making organization a difficult task.[11] Green replied that the Executive Council of the AFL had been considering his question and that action would probably be taken in the near future.[12] Some weeks later Green announced his intention of calling an AFL-CROM confer-

6. *Ibid.*
7. Green to Iglesias, April 25, 1925; GrCB.
8. Green to Iglesias, Feb. 25, 1925; GrCB.
9. Green to Morones, May 11, 1925; GrCB. Green to Iglesias, May 11, 1925; GrCB. Green to Iglesias, May 13, 1925; GrCB. Green to Iglesias, May 14. 1925; GrCB. Green to Iglesias, June 30, 1925; GrCB.
10. Green to Iglesias, July 15, 1925; GrCB.
11. Green to Clemente N. Idar, April 23, 1925; GrCB.
12. *Ibid.*

ence to deal with the matter,[13] and in mid-June he asked
Eduardo Moneda if he and his colleagues could attend an
immigration conference in Washington on June 23.[14] The
leaders of the CROM were willing to discuss the problem,
but as Morones could not leave Mexico at the time suggested,
August 27 was chosen instead.[15] In the meantime Green explained to the AFL Executive Council that his plan was to
control Mexican immigration through voluntary action on
the part of the Mexican government rather than through restrictive legislation on the part of the United States. Specifically, it was his intention to ask the leaders of the CROM to
persuade their government to limit the number of visas
granted to Mexican workers who planned to seek employment in the United States.[16]

The immigration conference was held in Washington on
August 27-28, 1925. Present were Green, Iglesias, Morones,
and Haberman. The attitude toward immigration which prevailed at this conference reflected the philosophy expounded
by Gompers at the Second Congress in 1919: a government
has the right to restrict or prohibit immigration when to do
so promotes the interests of the nation, but it also has the
responsibility of restricting emigration of its own citizens
when an influx of excess labor into another country would
be detrimental to the welfare of the people of that country.[17]
The delegates agreed that steps be taken to have the governments of the United States and Mexico accept this principle
of voluntary restriction of emigration.[18] They further agreed
that since it would take time and study to prepare a brief
supporting this principle, they would for the time being make

13. Green to Idar, May 13, 1925; GrCB.
14. Green to Eduardo Moneda, June 12, 1925; GrCB. Green to Moneda,
June 15, 1925; GrCB.
15. Green to Moneda, July 1, 1925; GrCB. Green to Morones, July 15, 1925;
GrCB.
16. AFL Executive Council Minutes, July 30, 1925.
17. *Proceedings*, 5th PAFL Cong., pp. 39-41. *Proceedings*, 2nd PAFL Cong.,
p. 55.
18. *Proceedings*, 5th PAFL Cong., p. 40.

every effort to see that immigrant workers join the unions in their fields and that they faithfully observe the rules of the labor organizations with which they might affiliate.[19] Green did not insist upon the adoption of the plan that he had discussed with the AFL Executive Council regarding the restriction of visas, although this was presumably the device that the Mexican government would be forced to use.

Only a few months after the immigration conference, the PAFL was faced with the revolt of the Roman Catholic Church against the Calles government. The revolt began on January 27, 1926, when the first of a series of protests by the Church against the anticlerical clauses of the Constitution of 1917 appeared in Mexico City's *El Universal*.[20] Subsequent protests were followed by the suspension of all religious services by the Church, an economic boycott directed by the Church, an armed rebellion fostered by the Church, and finally the murder of President-elect Alvaro Obregón by a young Roman Catholic fanatic. In March 1926, only a short time after the Church had begun its anti-Calles campaign, the AFL sent delegates to the CROM convention in Mexico City, and in a speech before this convention Calles gave the impression that the AFL was supporting him in the conflict,[21] which was by no means true. Actually both the AFL and the PAFL were successful in remaining aloof from the struggle. Green attempted to keep the issue out of the American labor movement by making no official pronouncements regarding the matter, although he eventually found it necessary to declare that the conflict had no relation to the labor movement, and as the connection of the AFL with the CROM through the PAFL was a purely economic one, the subject was not to be further discussed by the AFL.[22] Matthew Woll,

19. *Ibid.*, p. 41.
20. Mexico City *El Universal*, Jan. 27, 1926.
21. New York *Times*, March 2, 1926.
22. New York *Times*, Aug. 6, 1926. *Ibid.*, Aug. 12, 1926. *Ibid.*, Aug. 25, 1926.

the Roman Catholic president of the AFL Photoengravers Union who became the treasurer of the PAFL while the religious conflict was in progress, publicly announced that the AFL would continue to support the Mexican labor movement but would remain neutral in the church-state dispute.[23] The subject was never mentioned in the *American Federationist,* the official organ of the AFL, during the course of the conflict, and the PAFL found it easy to avoid discussion of the matter by citing a resolution adopted by its Fourth Congress which forbade any affiliated union to take part in a religious controversy.[24] Nevertheless, groups associated with the Roman Catholic Church in the United States made every effort to involve the labor movement. The editor of the Jesuit organ *America* refused to accept the neutrality proclaimed by the AFL and demanded that it take action against Calles.[25] *Columbia,* the official publication of the Knights of Columbus, included the AFL in its list of Calles supporters along with the Industrial Workers of the World, the Socialist party, the Socialist Workers party, the Workers [Communist] party, the Ku Klux Klan, and the Birth Control League.[26] This same publication criticized the AFL and the United States government for having aided in the creation of the radical Mexican government and it called upon them to recognize their error, confess their bad judgment, and make amends—[27] presumably by repudiating Calles. At only one time was there danger that the leadership would lose control of the situation and that was at the AFL annual convention in 1926 when James Fitzpatrick, a delegate to the convention, charged from the floor that the CROM was an instrument of Calles and that the Mexican government was "red." Matthew Woll quickly took the floor to deny the charge and to plead

23. New York *Times,* Aug. 16, 1926.
24. *Proceedings,* 4th PAFL Cong., p. 132.
25. *America,* Oct. 2, 1926, p. 583.
26. *Columbia,* Oct. 1926, p. 24.
27. *Ibid.,* Sept. 1926, p. 26.

with the convention not to let a religious issue split the AFL. Following his appeal, the convention showed its unity by reaffirming its support of the PAFL.[28]

While military activity in the Mexican church-state conflict was at its height, the fifth and last congress of the PAFL was held at AFL headquarters in Washington on July 18-23, 1927. This was the best-attended of all the PAFL congresses. Present were delegates representing labor movements in twelve countries: the United States, Mexico, Panama, Peru, Venezuela, Guatemala, Nicaragua, Honduras, the Dominican Republic, Cuba, Colombia, and Puerto Rico.[29] In addition, telegrams and letters expressing solidarity with the PAFL were received from national labor movements and individual organizations in Argentina, Haiti, Chile, El Salvador, Bolivia, Costa Rica, and Germany. Even the IFTU sent best wishes for success.[30] Such widespread interest in the PAFL had never been shown in the past.

No formal mention of the Church problem in Mexico was made during the course of the Fifth Congress, although the conflict continued. It was suggested, however, in the keynote address by William Green when he referred to the necessity of each nation preserving its basic freedoms, including freedom of conscience and the right to worship as one pleases without any restriction whatsoever.[31]

The report of the Executive Committee to the Fifth Congress contained sixteen items, only four of which are of more than passing importance: labor participation in the Pan-American Commercial Conference, oppression of the workers in Cuba, civil war in Nicaragua, and the conference on Mexican immigration into the United States discussed earlier in this chapter.

28. New York *Times*, Oct. 15, 1926.
29. *Proceedings*, 5th PAFL Cong., p. 19.
30. *Ibid.*, pp. 13-17.
31. *Ibid.*, p. 5.

Labor participation in the various international conferences sponsored by the Pan American Union had been sought by Gompers as far back as 1915, and we have already noted how he tried unsuccessfully to have the Second Pan-American Financial Conference in 1920 adopt a resolution providing for discussion at the Third Conference of problems relating to human welfare and the well-being of the working class.[32] Green had continued the policy of Gompers in respect to labor participation in conferences of this kind, and in accordance with a resolution adopted by the Fourth Congress of the PAFL he asked President Calvin Coolidge to include an AFL representative to the Third Pan-American Commercial Conference, which was to be held in 1927. Coolidge acceded to Green's request and asked him to nominate a delegate. Green suggested Matthew Woll, the treasurer of the PAFL at that time. Woll was consequently named by Secretary of State Frank B. Kellogg as a full-fledged delegate to the Third Conference, which met in Washington on May 2-5, 1927. Woll presented to the conference a resolution regarding the welfare of working people in the Americas which was adopted in the following form: "That in the program of topics to be discussed at future commercial conferences there be included the subject of improving the material standards of life and labor of the masses of the people of the respective countries so that by improving the conditions of labor production is fomented and consumption is increased, thereby contributing to the development of commerce."[33] This resolution was adopted unanimously. The resolution as originally phrased by Woll was in simple language, but the conference delegates felt that it should be reworded so that it would harmonize with the phraseology of the final report.[34]

The Executive Committee's report to the Fifth Congress

32. Cf. p. 69 above.
33. *Proceedings*, 5th PAFL Cong., p. 28.
34. *Ibid.*, pp. 27-29.

on Cuba dealt with the conflict that had arisen between the Cuban labor movement and the government of President Gerardo Machado. In 1925 a strike of Cuban railroad workers centered in the Camagüey sugar region succeeded in bringing transportation to a standstill. When it became apparent that the strikers were on the verge of winning, a campaign of terror against them was begun by Machado and the strike was broken. During this period reports of the brutality and terroristic methods of the Machado government were received by the PAFL from a number of sources, and after the strike had been broken similar reports continued to arrive. The result was that in February 1927 Green and Iglesias in a conference with Orestes Ferrar, the Cuban ambassador to the United States, attempted to bring pressure on Machado to adopt a more humane policy toward organized labor. After discussing the matter with Ferrar, Green handed him a list of crimes allegedly committed against persons in the Cuban labor movement by Machado. Within a few days Ferrar sent Green a detailed denial of all the charges listed. Ferrar tried to give the impression that Machado was sympathetic to organized labor, and he claimed that the difficulties that had arisen in Cuba were due entirely to a small number of foreign radicals who had taken advantage of the railroad strike to further their own ends. The real object of the radicals, Ferrar went on to say, was to bring about discord and revolution in Cuba which would spread to the mainland.[35] This oft-repeated explanation of violence toward organized labor by conservative governments was tacitly supported by the Cuban delegates to the Fifth Congress when they introduced a resolution stating that the Machado government permitted labor organization and activity provided they did not harm the government or the people of Cuba. Adoption of this resolution would have been tantamount to recognition if not

35. *Ibid.,* pp. 42-57.

support of the corrupt Machado regime by the PAFL. Probably for this reason the resolutions committee recommended that it be referred to the Executive Committee for consideration, and this was the action taken.[36]

At the time of the Fifth Congress the Coolidge government was busily occupied in an attempt to maintain in power in Nicaragua the corrupt government of conservative Adolfo Díaz. Strong measures had been taken by the United States, and at the very beginning of the Fifth Congress Nicaraguan delegate Salomón de la Selva asked for and was granted a suspension of the rules while he read a long resolution relating to Nicaragua. In it he quoted an Associated Press dispatch telling of the killing of an estimated three hundred persons in Ocotal, Nicaragua, by United States military forces which were said to have employed five bombing planes in the attack on the defenseless town. The resolution expressed sympathy for the Nicaraguans, emphatically protested the action of the United States armed forces, and demanded the immediate withdrawal of all American military personnel from Nicaragua. This resolution was referred to the resolutions committee for preferential consideration.[37] Later, the congress adopted three resolutions relating to Nicaragua, one of which called on the State Department to withdraw all American troops from that country.[38]

Toward the end of the Fifth Congress a dispute arose which threatened to assume serious proportions over a resolution jointly proposed by the Venezuelan and Nicaraguan delegations and relating to the Monroe Doctrine. The text of the original resolution is not available, but the substitute resolution drafted by the resolutions committee under the chairmanship of Matthew Woll is sufficiently critical of the Doctrine to suggest that the original—which was apparently the

36. *Ibid.*, pp. 120-121.
37. *Ibid.*, pp. 23-25.
38. *Ibid.*, pp. 92-93.

work of Salomón de la Selva—was couched in the most condemnatory terms. For the first time since the heated dispute over the IWW at the Laredo Conference there was manifested among the delegates a division of feeling of the kind that destroys organizations. It was not the resolution itself which was in dispute as much as it was the Monroe Doctrine. The radical delegates contended that the Doctrine was a thing of evil, while the delegates from the United States and their supporters insisted that it had protected the weak Latin-American nations from greedy European powers. After a long discussion in which the delegates expressed themselves in a vociferous manner, the substitute resolution was adopted. It condemned the stand of the United States that American military power should be used to protect the property of American citizens in Latin-America, and it supported the principle that the property of a foreigner in any Latin-American country should be given protection equal to, but not greater than, that accorded a citizen of the country in question.[39]

The last resolution adopted by the Fifth Congress referred to the resignation of Chester M. Wright, who had been English-language secretary of the PAFL since the death of John Murray. In a letter of resignation in which he expressed best wishes for the success of the organization, Wright declared that there was not sufficient work to keep two secretaries occupied. His resignation was formally accepted by the congress after Green had made a short statement in appreciation of his services.[40] Henceforth, Iglesias was to be the sole secretary of the organization.

As the Fifth Congress drew to a close, Peruvian delegate Luis Ríos Castell moved that the present office holders be re-elected in a body. Delegate Ricardo A. Martínez of the expatriate Unión Obrera Venezolana of New York, who had

39. *Ibid.*, pp. 123-124.
40. *Ibid.*, pp. 134-135.

led the fight against the Monroe Doctrine, suggested that Morones be nominated for the presidency, but Morones refused the nomination with the explanation that he could not establish himself in Washington, where the headquarters of the PAFL would continue to be located. There being no other nominees, Green, Morones, Iglesias, and Woll were elected president, vice-president, secretary, and treasurer respectively.[41]

Although both the AFL and the PAFL had been able to keep from becoming publicly involved in the religious conflict which was still harassing the Mexican government, they were unable to refuse assistance to the CROM following the murder of Alvaro Obregón by a young Roman Catholic fanatic on July 17, 1928. In recent years Morones had openly shown a difference of opinion with Obregón on several points relating to the welfare of the country, and with the death of Obregón the enemies of Morones and the CROM seized on these differences as a pretext to destroy Morones and his followers. Chief among these enemies of Morones were the *agraristas,* the *obregonistas,* and the Church. Immediately following the assassination, the danger to the CROM leaders was sufficiently great for them to seek refuge in the Ciudadela; and within a short time Morones, Celestino Gasca, and Eduardo Moneda, the chiefs of the Department of Industry, Commerce, and Labor, the Ordnance Department, and the Government Printing Shops respectively resigned their government positions at the suggestion of President Calles. The situation was critical, and on August 8 Morones wired to Iglesias to come to Mexico.

Iglesias arrived in Mexico City on August 31 and established headquarters in the Hotel Regis. Accompanied by Ricardo Treviño and Cayetano Ruiz, both of whom had long been associated with the PAFL, Iglesias proceeded without

41. *Ibid.,* p. 138.

delay to the home of Morones in Tlalpan, a small town about five miles south of the capital. There he found assembled the majority of Mexico's outstanding labor leaders, including a number of persons who had been active in the leadership of the PAFL since its founding. Morones told Iglesias of the trials that he and his colleagues had undergone since the murder of Obregón and of the accusation which had been made against them of being psychologically and intellectually responsible for the crime. The object of this accusation, Morones explained, was to create a great mass emotional upsurge which could be utilized to justify attacks upon, and possibly the assassination of, the leaders of Mexican labor along with the destruction of the Partido Laborista. Morones asked Iglesias to make a thorough investigation upon which to base a report to Green which, through the PAFL, could be publicized throughout the world. Morones also gave Iglesias a number of documents supporting the innocence of the Mexican labor movement in the assassination. Among these documents was a copy of the hitherto secret agreement of 1919 made between Obregón and the representatives of the Partido Laborista in which Obregón agreed to carry out a prolabor program in return for support from the Partido Laborista. The full text of this agreement as translated by Iglesias is as follows:

POINTS which, with the character of PRIVATE COVENANT, WERE presented to ALVARO OBREGON, as a candidate of the Working Class to occupy the Presidency of the Republic.

I. Our desire is that a Ministry, known as the Ministry of Labor, should be created to solve especially everything regarding the interests of the workingmen; and that a person identified with the moral and material needs of the workingmen be in charge of same.

II. That while the purposes of Point I are being undertaken, a person should be appointed who will have the requirements referred to in that point, to the position of Minister of Industry, Commerce, and Labor.

III. That a person be appointed to the Secretaryship of Agriculture and Fomento, sufficiently capable in that branch, and that all reasonable suggestions that he might make in his capacity, should be favorably considered.

IV. That in the appointment of the persons referred to in Points I, II, and III, the opinion of the representatives of the Political Party, which has been formed at the initiative of the subscribers, should be taken into consideration; a requirement of the former being that the persons recommended should have the proper and necessary qualifications for the holding of the office.

V. That as soon as the LABOR LAW is approved its promulgation should be immediate, and the Executive Power of the Union should exert all efforts for the best fulfillment of the same.

VI. That the legal personality of the Central Committee of the Mexican Federation of Labor [the CROM] be recognized, to deal directly with the Ministry of Labor, or in any case with the Executive Power of the Union in all matters regarding the Labor organizations of the Republic.

VII. That at least a meeting day each week should be designated to carry into effect the above point, except when special cases might indicate a greater need.

VIII. That all necessary facilities be extended in order to carry out all the agreements tending toward the welfare and cultural progress of the workingmen which have been decided upon in the Labor Congresses held in the cities of Saltillo, Coah., and Zacatecas, Zac., as well as those which might be arrived at in the future Congresses.

IX. That the opinions of the representatives of the Labor Organizations of the country be taken into consideration when reforms or procedures of general interest are to be put into practice.

X. That all necessary facilities be given for labor propaganda and labor organization in the country.

XI. That all necessary facilities be given for the work of labor unification outside of the Republic in order to strengthen the relations between our people and other people and thus be able to avoid any international peril which might arise.

This document was signed in Mexico City on August 6, 1919, by the following persons, most of whom were intimately associated with the PAFL at one time or another: Samuel O. Yúdico, Salvador Alvarez, Reynaldo Cervantes Torres, José Lópes Cortés, Celestino Gasca, Eduardo Moneda, A. Polo, Ezequiel Salcedo, Luis Morones, Juan B. Fonseca, José F. Gutiérrez, and Alvaro Obregón.[42]

For a week or more following his meeting with Morones, Iglesias talked with numerous persons about the current crisis. Among these were workingmen, government officials, military leaders, *obregonistas, agraristas,* and *anti-reeleccionistas* as well as Mexican and foreign writers, businessmen, reporters, and so on. His investigation convinced him that neither the Church nor the labor movement was responsible for the murder of Obregón.[43]

Before leaving Mexico, Iglesias had a three-hour conference with President Calles. The President gave him a frank account of the most intimate problems of the Mexican government, the various political alignments, and the question of the generals. He discussed in considerable detail the ramifications of the problem that had arisen and how he had been able to prevent civil war by getting the support of the various factions in the army. He told of his cross-examination of José León de Toral, the murderer of Obregón, and how he was convinced by the behavior of Toral that neither the Church nor the CROM was implicated. The conclusions of Calles regarding

42. Iglesias to Green, Oct. 4, 1928: "Report of My Extraordinary Trip to Mexico from August 23 to September 21, 1928"; IP.
43. *Ibid.*

the attack that had been made on Morones and the CROM were essentially the same as those which had been expressed by Morones himself. At no time did Calles mention directly the church-state conflict, which was now at its height, nor did he comment on the attacks of the Church in the United States on himself as well as Morones. Iglesias himself observed the same discreet silence in the forty-four-page report which he prepared for William Green upon his return to the United States.[44]

Except for the events already related in this chapter, there was no activity of great importance between the closing of the Fifth Congress and the call to the Sixth Congress, which was sent out in April 1929. Havana had already been chosen by the Fifth Congress as the meeting place,[45] and in the call the Executive Committee set the date for January 6, 1930.[46] In July 1929 a supplement to the call was issued which contained a three-page suggestion by Matthew Woll that the establishment of a World Federation of Labor to oppose the IFTU be discussed at the Sixth Congress. The reason given by Woll for this suggestion was that the IFTU did not allow complete autonomy to its affiliated federations, and it could therefore by a majority vote force its entire membership into action that a minority might oppose.[47] This was the feature of the IFTU that had led Gompers to remain aloof down through the years.

On October 30, 1929, the Executive Committee of the PAFL announced in a special bulletin that the Sixth Congress would be postponed. The relationship of this announcement to the stock market crash of the preceding day is not clear, for there was no mention of this event in the announcement. The Executive Committee gave two reasons for the

44. *Ibid.*
45. *Proceedings*, 5th PAFL Cong., p. 148.
46. Call to the Sixth Congress to be held in Havana on the first Monday in January 1930, dated April 1929; IP.
47. *A las organizaciones obreras y prensa de todos los países Pan-Americanos*, a mimeographed PAFL press release dated July 1929; IP.

postponement: first, the American Federation of Labor had planned for the immediate future an extensive organizing campaign in the southern part of the United States; second, word had been received from Latin America of economic and other problems which made postponement of the congress desirable. The announcement made it clear that the postponement was temporary, and that the Sixth Congress would be held when a date suitable to all concerned could be found.[48]

At some time during the first nine months of 1930, the Executive Committee in a letter to all Pan-American labor organizations suggested that the congress be held in January 1931, but responses favoring the meeting were received from only six countries: Cuba, Mexico, Venezuela, Guatemala, Haiti, and the Dominican Republic. Honduras replied that it probably would not send a delegation because of lack of funds, and Colombia asked for a postponement of another year because of a recent change in government administration there.[49] By December 1930 both Bolivia and Peru had joined Colombia in asking for another postponement, although Argentina and Ecuador had said that they would give the matter consideration. No definite answer had been received from Brazil, Nicaragua, El Salvador, Panama, Paraguay, Costa Rica, Chile, and Uruguay.[50] Months went by without conclusive action until late in August 1931 when Green informed Iglesias that there could be no congress in the immediate future as the PAFL budget which he had recently submitted to the AFL Executive Council had been refused consideration because of the depression and the consequent scarcity of funds.[51] But the AFL did not intend to

48. *A los centros de trabajadores organizados de las repúblicas americanas,* a mimeographed letter by the Executive Committee of the PAFL, dated Oct. 30, 1929; IP.

49. The date of the letter referred to is not available, as it is only mentioned in a report in the *Proceedings,* 50th AFL Conv., p. 122.

50. Confederación Obrera Pan-Americana Informe Especial, diciembre 1930; IP.

51. Green to Iglesias, Aug. 28, 1931; IP.

abandon the PAFL altogether, for at its annual convention held in October 1931, its Committee on International Relations stated that the Executive Council would appoint a delegation to the Sixth Congress whenever the Latin-American organizations were ready to meet.[52] Still another year passed, and in his report to the fifty-second annual convention of the AFL in 1932, Iglesias could only say, without citing cases, that the PAFL had been able during the past year to be helpful to Latin-American countries "on numerous occasions," although it had been impossible to hold the Sixth Congress because of the depression, political revolutions, and military uprisings.[53] Darkness seems to have settled over the Western Hemisphere and during 1933 and 1934 the decline of the PAFL continued. At the AFL convention in 1934 Iglesias reported that during the depression years the labor movements in Latin America had been in a stagnant state but he hoped that the PAFL would soon resume its meetings.[54] The following year the PAFL was hardly more than mentioned, but in 1936 it appeared that there was some hope of a revival. Iglesias reported in that year to the AFL convention that a circular had been sent to the unions in Latin America asking for their opinion regarding sending out a call to the Sixth Congress. The circular had been "well received," as Iglesias put it, by unions in Argentina, Colombia, Chile, Costa Rica, Ecuador, El Salvador, Guatemala, Venezuela, Mexico, and Cuba.[55] In the meantime, the labor movement in the Dominican Republic, which had shown such promise, had been destroyed by President Rafael Leónidas Trujillo.[56]

The optimistic tone of the 1936 report by Iglesias indicated only a momentary brightening of the picture, for the follow-

52. *Proceedings*, 51st AFL Conv., p. 148.
53. *Proceedings*, 52nd AFL Conv., p. 115.
54. *Proceedings*, 54th AFL Conv., p. 170, 724.
55. *Proceedings*, 56th AFL Conv., p. 196.
56. *Ibid.*, p. 197.

ing year the PAFL was completely ignored by the delegates to the AFL convention. In 1937, however, correspondence between Iglesias and Juan Arévalo, the secretary-general of the Buró Representativo de Gremios Afiliados, indicated that some interest in the PAFL still remained in Cuba,[57] although Iglesias' reminder to Arévalo that the Cuban unions had not paid their quotas for "many years"[58] was a pathetic suggestion of the condition of the PAFL.

From September 5 through September 8, 1938, there was held in Mexico City under radical auspices the Congreso Obrero Latinoamericano.[59] This congress of exclusively Latin-American delegates formed a new organization, the Confederación de Trabajadores de América Latina and established its headquarters in Mexico City.[60] The organization did not include in its membership labor groups from the United States or Canada, although John L. Lewis of the Congress of Industrial Organizations had supported Vicente Lombardo Toledano—the pro-Communist Mexican leader of the movement—in its formation[61] and had been a fraternal delegate to the Congreso Obrero.[62]

The formation of the Confederación de Trabajadores de América Latina indicated that a new trend in Latin-American labor organization was beginning and that the future would see a struggle between liberalism and radicalism in the Americas. The split in the AFL and the consequent formation of the leftist CIO had already shown that the United States itself was not exempt from this trend.

In October 1938, the AFL at its annual convention decided

57. Juan Arévalo to Iglesias, March 8, 1937; IP. Iglesias to Arévalo, March 22, 1937; IP.
58. Iglesias to Arévalo, March 22, 1937; IP.
59. *Congreso obrero latinoamericano: Ciudad de México, 5 al 8 de septiembre de 1938* (n.p., n.d.), p. 69; a copy of this printed report is in the Library of Congress.
60. *Ibid.*
61. New York *Times*, June 28, 1938.
62. *Congreso obrero latinoamericano: Ciudad de México, 5 al 8 de septiembre, de 1938*, pp. 48-50.

that an attempt should be made to rebuild the PAFL. This decision was undoubtedly in response to the formation of the Confederación de Trabajadores de América Latina, the success of which could mean the end of AFL influence in Latin America and especially in Mexico. The convention proposed that an exploratory commission be sent to Latin America to determine the number of "free"[63] labor unions remaining there. If it appeared that there was a possibility of success, the Sixth Congress would be called.[64]

In accordance with the decision of the AFL convention, the PAFL Executive Committee made a survey by correspondence of sentiment for convening the Sixth Congress, and late in 1939 it sent Iglesias on a reorganizing tour which had been planned to carry him to many parts of Latin America. After attending a meeting of the International Labor Organization in Havana, he proceeded to Mexico. There he became seriously ill and, forced to abandon his tour, he returned to Washington, where he died on December 5, 1939.[65] This ended the campaign for reorganization of the PAFL.

The year following the death of Iglesias, Morones tried to revive the interest of the AFL in the organization, but his attempt was half-hearted and received little attention.[66] Still, the PAFL was not dissolved. The office of secretary, which had been left vacant by the death of Iglesias, was combined with that of treasurer and given to Matthew Woll, although he had no knowledge of the Spanish language.[67] At the last AFL convention held before the United States entered World War II, there was a spiritless discussion of the PAFL,[68] but by now it was clear to everyone that the organization was dead.

63. Presumably the word "free" as used here refers to those labor organizations not under the influence or control of communist or pro-communist elements or to unions in dictator-controlled countries.
64. *Proceedings*, 58th AFL Conv., p. 200.
65. *Proceedings*, 59th AFL Conv., p. 224. *Proceedings*, 60th AFL Conv., p. 218.
66. *Proceedings*, 60th AFL Conv., p. 218.
67. *Proceedings*, 61st AFL Conv., p. 219.
68. *Ibid.*

The Pan-American Federation of Labor had been in existence for twenty-three years by 1941, but its active life had not exceeded ten or twelve years. During this period it had to a limited degree attained three of the four objectives set for it by the Second Congress. These three objectives were: the establishment of better understanding and better relations between the peoples of the Pan-American countries; the protection and advancement of the rights, interests, and wellbeing of the people living in this area; and the cultivation of favorable and friendly relations between the labor movements and the people in all the countries of the Western Hemisphere.[69] Its greatest successes had been in connection with Mexico, for there is no question but that better relations had been established between the people of Mexico and the people of the United States, the welfare of the Mexican people had been promoted, and friendly relations between the CROM and the Mexican people had been cultivated. The success of the PAFL in nations other than Mexico had not been great, but it had been substantial.

It cannot be said with absolute certainty that the PAFL was the decisive factor in any of the major events in which it played a part, but it must be recognized that it contributed much to the victory of the Nicaraguan liberals in the 1924 presidential election, the termination of United States military rule in the Dominican Republic, the recognition by the United States of the Obregón government, the election of Calles in 1924, and the crushing of the de la Huerta revolt.

Perhaps the greatest success of the PAFL was in areas less spectacular than the ones just listed. At its congresses it established by resolution a wide variety of common aims for Pan-American labor such as the eight-hour day; prohibition of child labor; freedom of speech, press, and assembly; free and compulsory education for children; the right of labor to organize and strike; unification of labor on a national scale;

69. Cf. p. 57 above.

support of the League of Nations; solidarity of Pan-American labor; utilization of all idle lands; low cost, hygienic housing for workers on credit at a low interest rate; government-sponsored higher education for workers; a wage scale sufficiently high to allow the common people some of the luxuries of life; workmen's compensation; support of prolabor governments; opposition to tyrannical governments; non-participation in political and religious controversies by trade unions; and labor representation in the diplomatic service of all Pan-American nations. Furthermore, at its congresses union men from economically and culturally backward countries came in contact with labor leaders from more highly unionized nations having an advanced culture, notably the United States and Mexico, who gave them a deeper insight into labor problems and a feeling of "belonging" which contributed to labor solidarity on a hemispheric scale.

The PAFL failed to reach only one of the objectives listed by the Second Congress, and that was the establishment of better working conditions for workers migrating from one country to another, and especially Mexican workers migrating into the United States. A resolution dealing with this subject was adopted by the Second Congress,[70] but it apparently was never implemented by any of the PAFL affiliates.

Despite its commendable list of accomplishments, it must be recognized that the PAFL was only a limited success. This is shown by its failure to expand into a truly hemispheric organization, by the short term of its active life, and by the eventual rise of a rival organization, the Confederación de Trabajadores de América Latina.

The decline and end of the PAFL were due to a number of causes, chief among which was an ideological difference existing between the leaders of the AFL and the trade unionists of Latin America. Gompers, after some indecision

70. *Proceedings,* 2nd PAFL Cong., p. 62.

in his early years, had adopted the philosophy of coexistence of capital and labor. He had concluded that labor in a free contest with capital could obtain its just share of the products of society by using its traditional economic weapons, especially the strike and the boycott, in conjunction with its political power. He had definitely rejected the idea of the destruction of capitalism and he had likewise rejected the idea of a labor party. This philosophy became the common property of AFL leaders during the time of Gompers and has persisted down to the present time; and since the future of the AFL is dependent upon the existence of capitalism, we find that the AFL has been one of the most bitter enemies of those persons and groups who have sought to destroy the free enterprise system. The Latin-American trade unionists, on the other hand, tended to support the ideas of the radical left with the ultimate destruction of the capitalist order as their basic objective. This irreconcilable ideological difference was among the reasons why the national labor organizations of Argentina, Chile, and Uruguay did not affiliate with the PAFL.

Closely linked to this ideological difference was the fear of what the Latin-American workers called *monroismo obrero*, the domination of the Latin-American trade-union movement by organized labor in the United States, specifically the AFL. To many Latin Americans the PAFL was little more than an arm of the United States government, a view that had been fostered by the moral and financial support given the organization at its inception.

Subordinate to these two reasons were the low degree of industrial development in Latin America; the immaturity and sometimes virtual absence of trade-union movements in countries like Paraguay and Honduras; the failure of the PAFL to find a satisfactory solution to the problem of the exchange of union cards; the refusal of the PAFL to recognize intellectuals as delegates to its congresses; the domination of the organization by the AFL-CROM machine; the decline of the CROM; the split in the AFL; and the economic depression of the 1930's. In addition, the PAFL failed to evaluate properly the world-wide upsurge of radicalism which emphasized political rather than economic action as a cure for the workers' ills and which regarded the strike and other weapons of labor as means of gaining control of the state and not as devices for gaining limited economic objectives. But perhaps most important of all was the inability of the PAFL throughout its history to recognize that times were changing and that the radicalism of the Latins was deeply ingrained. The Pan-American Federation of Labor was based on concepts which had made of the American Federation of Labor a powerful weapon in the conflict between capital and labor in the United States during the decades between the 1880's and World War I. But in a new era and in a Latin-American environment an organization based on these concepts could not endure.

# Bibliography

The greater part of the material used in this book is from the manuscript collections listed below. The most extensive of these collections is composed of over three hundred bound volumes of the correspondence of Samuel Gompers. This is the collection commonly referred to as the Gompers Copybooks. It contains over three hundred thousand letters and telegrams written by Gompers over a period of approximately thirty years. The vast majority of letters in the Gompers Copybooks were written by Gompers, but a small number of them were written by other persons.

Equally extensive and consisting of incoming letters to Gompers as well as a large number of documentary papers is the collection on microfilm which may conveniently be referred to as the Gompers Microfilms. Both the Gompers Copybooks and the Gompers Microfilms contain a small amount of material not related to labor, although there is remarkably little biographical material in either collection.

The Iglesias Papers make up a collection of great value to students of Puerto Rican and Latin-American history. This collection includes what remains of the records of the Pan-American Federation of Labor.

The other collections listed are less extensive than those discussed above. The John Murray Collection includes a number of notebooks, but it contains few manuscripts.

The less important collections listed call for no special comment.

For convenience in footnoting, the various manuscript collections have been abbreviated as shown below.

## I. *Manuscripts*

American Federation of Labor Executive Council Minutes, abbreviated "AFL Executive Council Minutes." Headquarters of the American Federation of Labor–Congress of Industrial Organizations, Washington, D. C.

George Creel Papers, abbreviated "GCP-LC." Library of Congress, Washington, D. C.

Records of the Committee on Public Information, abbreviated "CPI-NA." National Archives, Washington, D. C.

Department of Labor Records, abbreviated "DL-NA." National Archives, Washington, D. C.

Gompers Microfilms, abbreviated "GM." Headquarters of the American Federation of Labor–Congress of Industrial Organizations, Washington, D. C.

Gompers Copybooks, abbreviated "GCB." Headquarters of the American Federation of Labor–Congress of Industrial Organizations, Washington, D. C.

William Green Copybooks, abbreviated "GrCB." Headquarters of the American Federation of Labor–Congress of Industrial Organizations, Washington, D. C.

John Murray Collection, abbreviated "JMC." Bancroft Library, University of California, Berkeley, California.

John Murray Papers, abbreviated "JMP." Mrs. Ethel Duffy Turner, Cuernavaca, Morelos, México.

State Department Records, abbreviated "SD-NA." National Archives, Washington, D. C.

Woodrow Wilson Papers, abbreviated "WP-LC." Library of Congress, Washington, D. C.

Santiago Iglesias Papers, abbreviated "IP." Mrs. Igualdad Iglesias de Pagán, Santurce, Puerto Rico.

## II. *Documents*

The *Proceedings* of the various annual conventions of the American Federation of Labor.

The *Proceedings* of the various congresses of the Pan-American Federation of Labor.

## III. *Newspapers*

The New York *Times*, 1915-1940.
The New York *Call*, 1916-1920.
Mexico City *El Universal*, January 27, 1926.
San Antonio, Texas, *The Pan-American Labor Press: El Obrero Panamericano*, 1918.

## IV. *Books*

ANGEL PERAL, MIGUEL. *Diccionario biográfico mexicano* (México, 1944).
ANON. *Congreso obrero latinoamericano: Ciudad de México, 5 al 8 de septiembre de 1938* (n.p., n.d.).
ANSEJO, CONRADO, ED. *Quien es quien en Puerto Rico* (San Juan, 1933-34).
CLINE, HOWARD F. *The United States and Mexico* (Cambridge, 1953).
CREEL, GEORGE. *Complete Report of the Chairman of the Committee on Public Information: 1917: 1918: 1919* (Washington, 1920).
GOMPERS, SAMUEL. *Seventy Years of Life and Labor: An Autobiography* (New York, 1925; 2 vols.).
KARSON, MARC. *American Labor Unions and Politics: 1900-1918* (Carbondale, Ill., 1958).
LÓPEZ APARICIO, ALFONSO. *El movimiento obrero en México: antecedentes, desarrollo y tendencias* (México, 1952).
LORWIN, LEWIS S. *Labor and Internationalism* (New York, 1929).
MOCK, JAMES R., and CEDRIC LARSON. *Words That Won the War* (Princeton, 1939).
POBLETE TRONCOSO, MOISÉS. *El movimiento obrero latinoamericano* (México, 1946).
REED, LOUIS S. *The Labor Philosophy of Samuel Gompers* (New York and London, 1930).
STIMSON, GRACE HEILMAN. *The Rise of the Labor Movement in Los Angeles* (Berkeley and Los Angeles, 1955).
TAFT, PHILIP. *The A. F. of L. in the Time of Gompers* (New York, 1957).
VILENKIN, YA. *Panamerikanskaya federatsiya truda* (Moscow, 1929).

## V. *Articles and Editorials*

ANON. "Appeal to U. S. Workers," *International Labor Forum* (New York), no month, 1916.

BRADY, PETER J., and ANTHONY McANDREW. "Puerto Rico obrero ante el pueblo y gobierno americano," *Justicia*, 21 de junio de 1920, pp. 12-17.

Editorial, *America*, Oct. 2, 1926, p. 583.

Editorial, *Columbia*, Oct. 1926, p. 24.

GOMPERS, SAMUEL. "United States—Mexican Labor: Their Relations," *American Federationist*, Aug. 1916, p. 7.

IGLESIAS PANTÍN, SANTIAGO. "Recuerdo de John Murray," *Justicia*, 19 de enero de 1920, p. 5.

REED, JOHN. "The Convention of the Dead," *Liberator*, Aug. 1919, pp. 12-20.

VARGAS, CANUTO A. "El legado de John Murray," *Justicia*, 11 de noviembre de 1920, p. 11.

# Index